Dot Markers A

ABC Numbers & Shapes

ABC
123
& Shapes

BIG Guided Dots

This book belongs to:

Color This dots

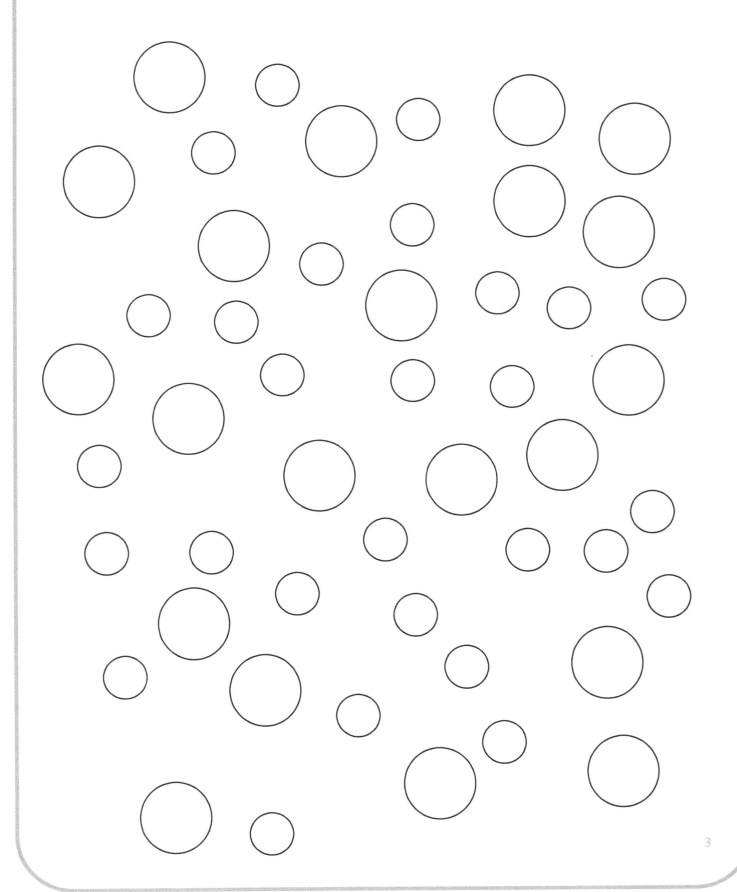

Color the following letters From A to Z

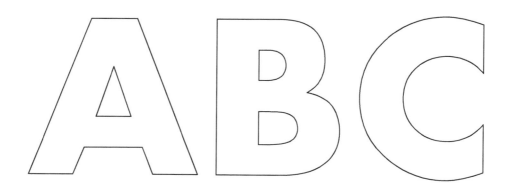

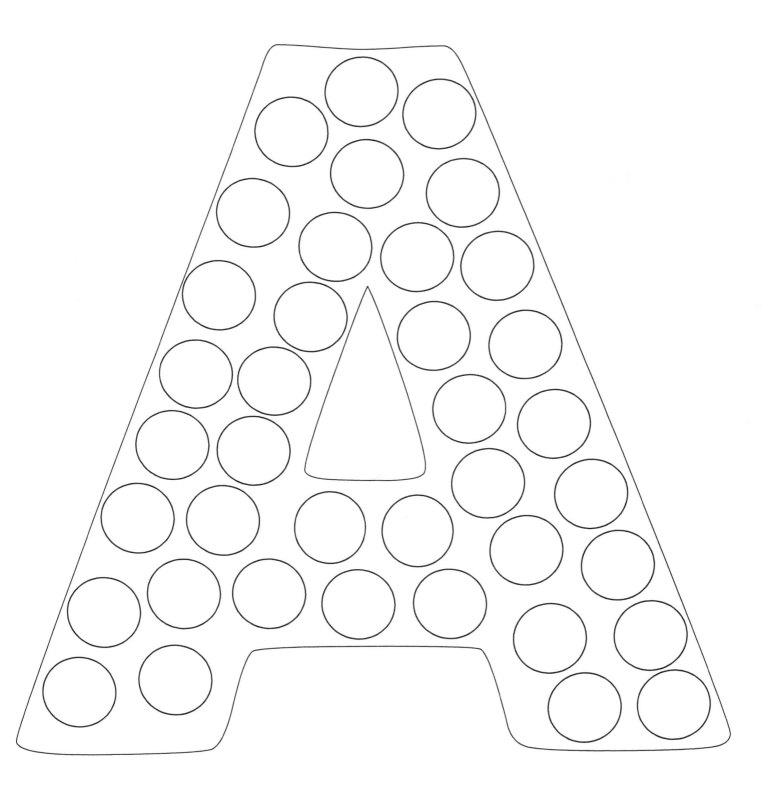

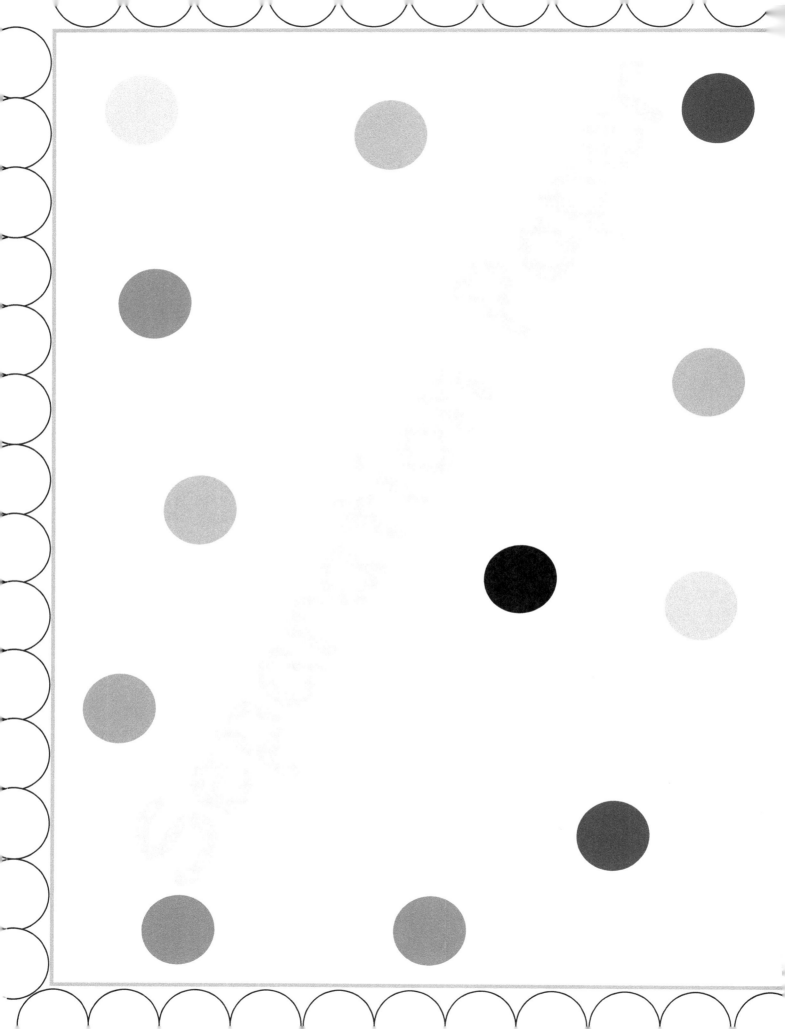

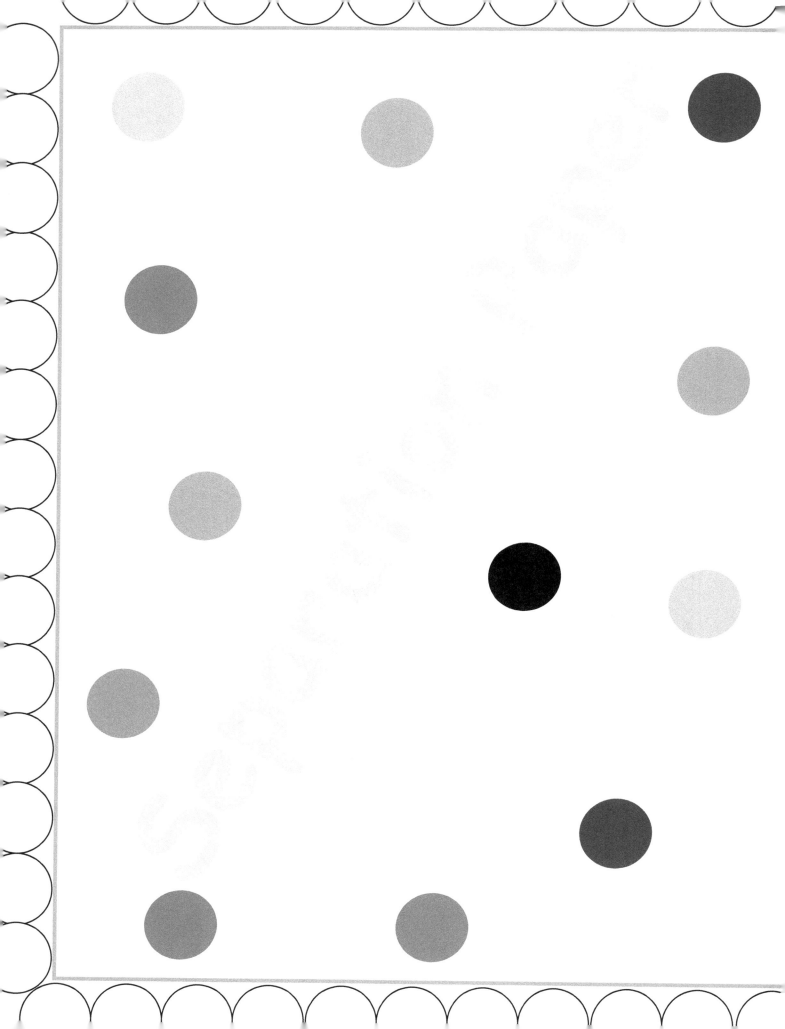

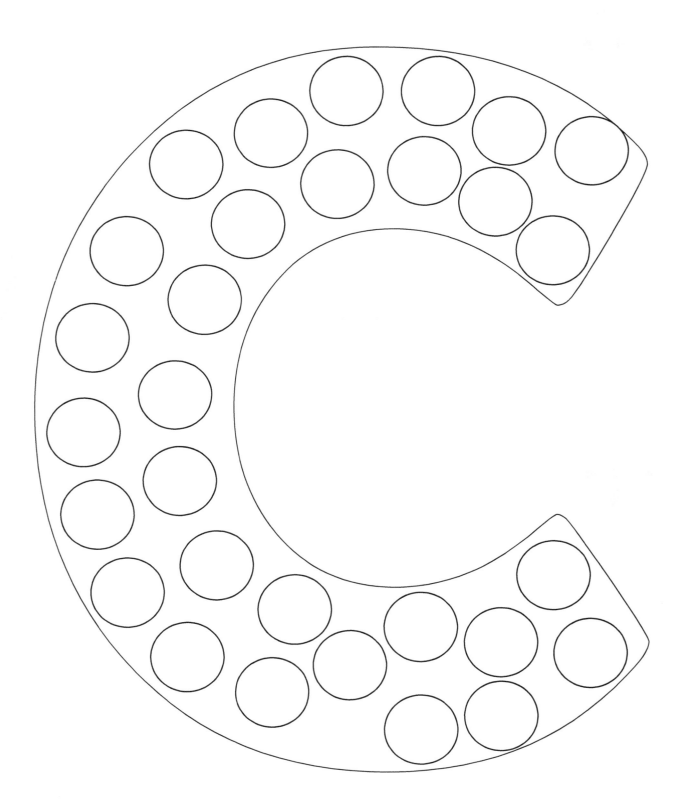

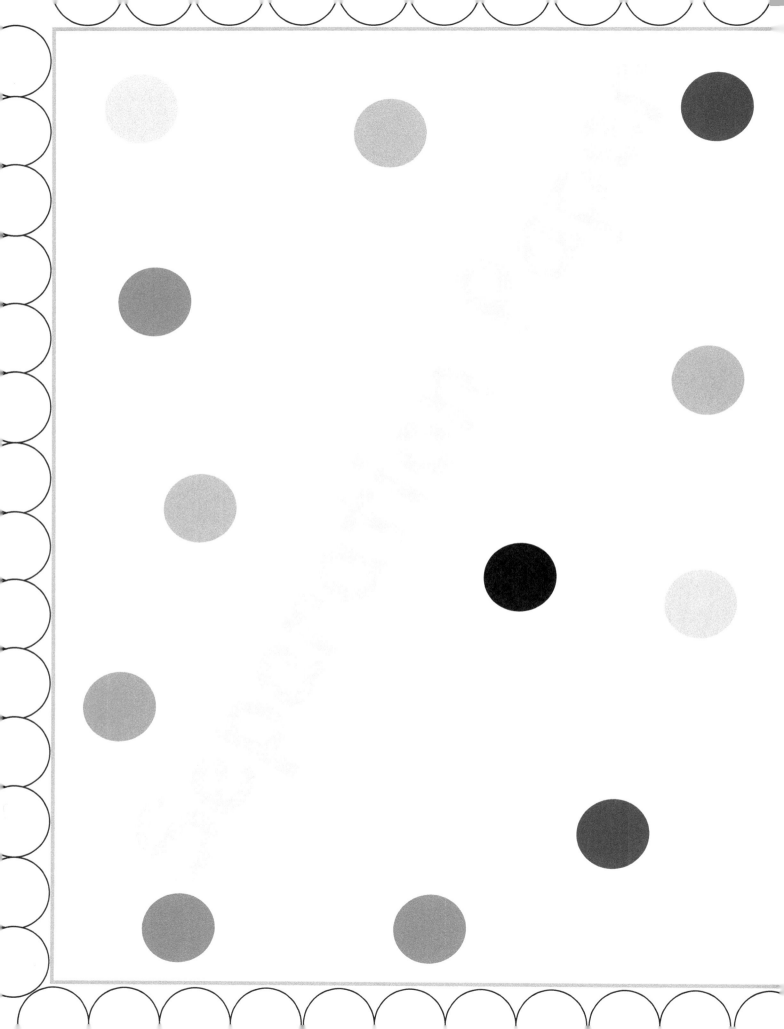

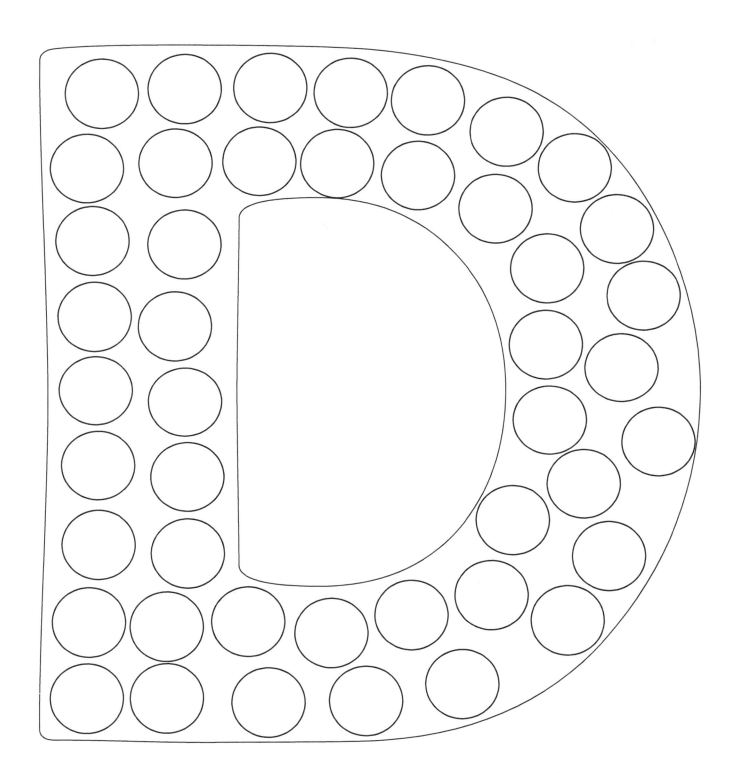

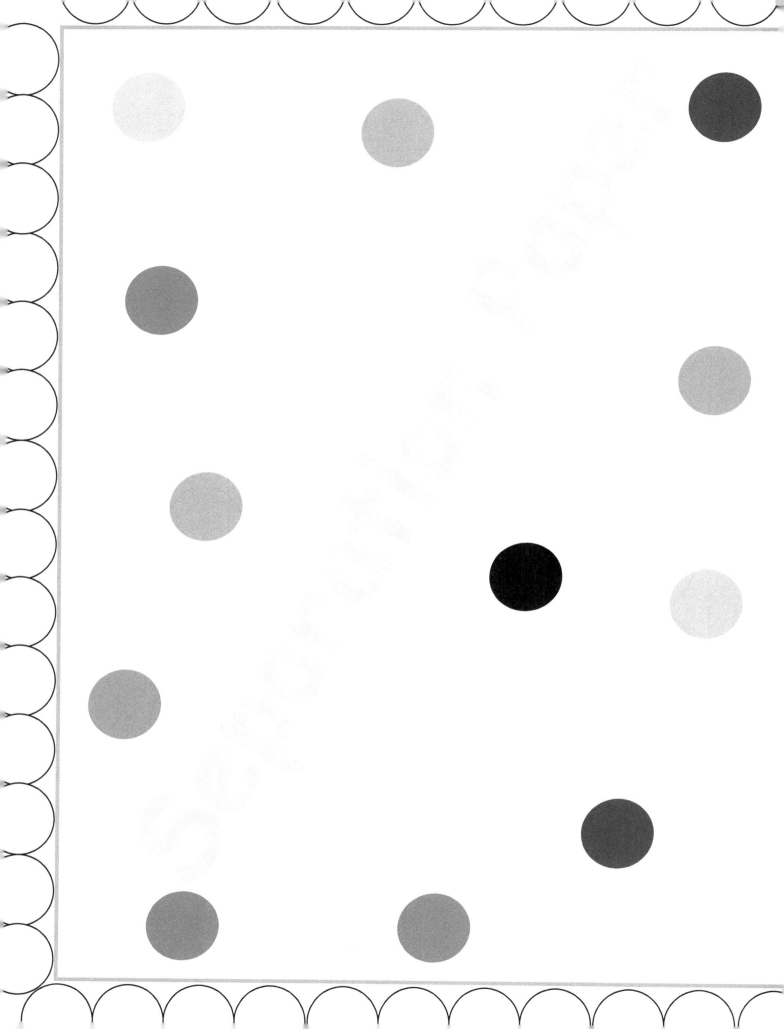

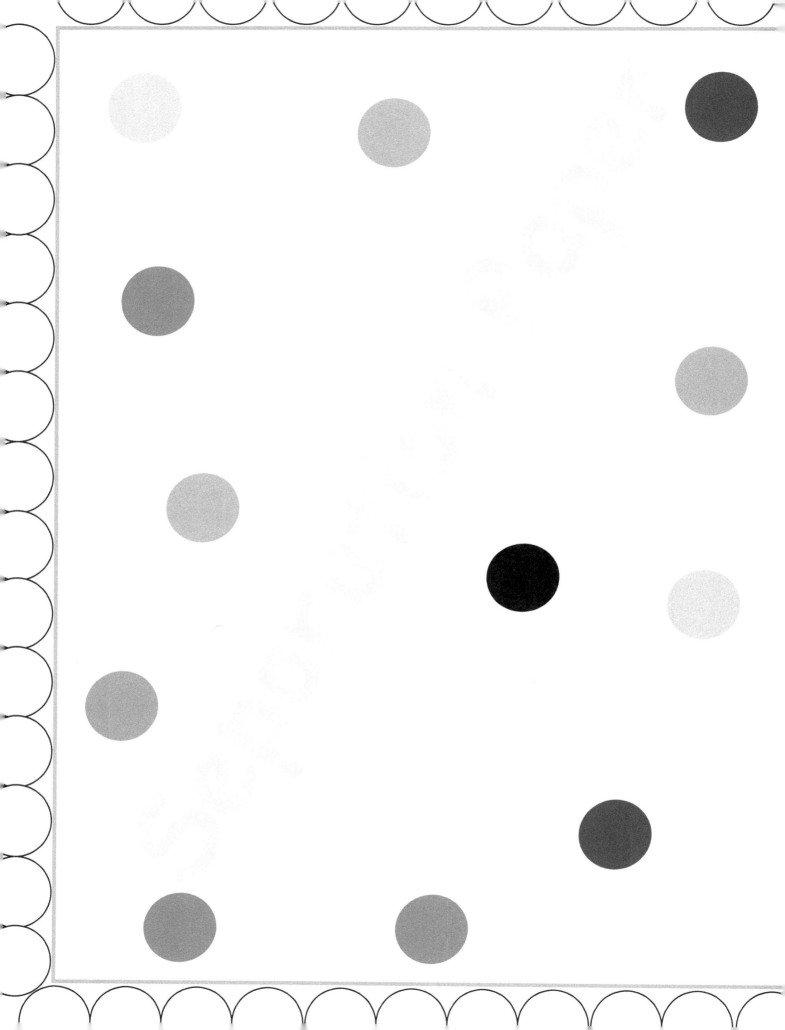

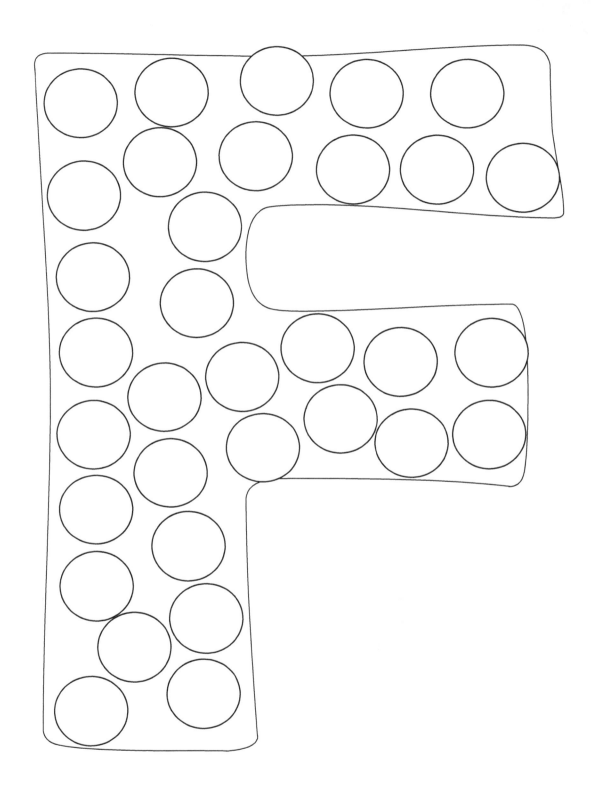

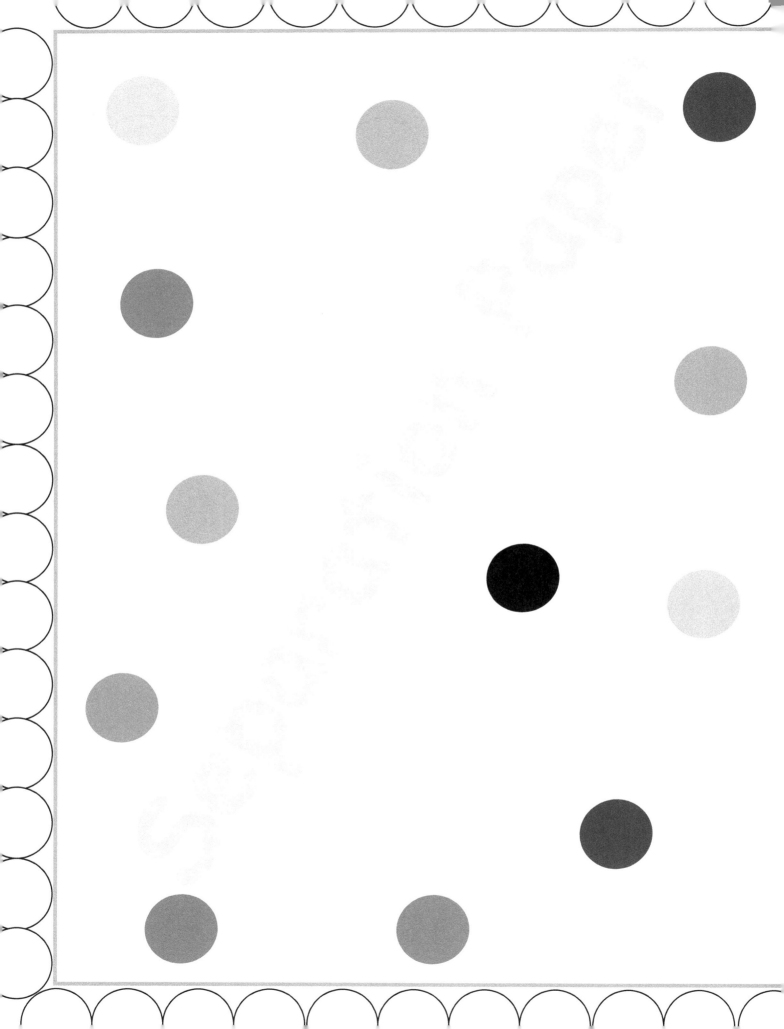

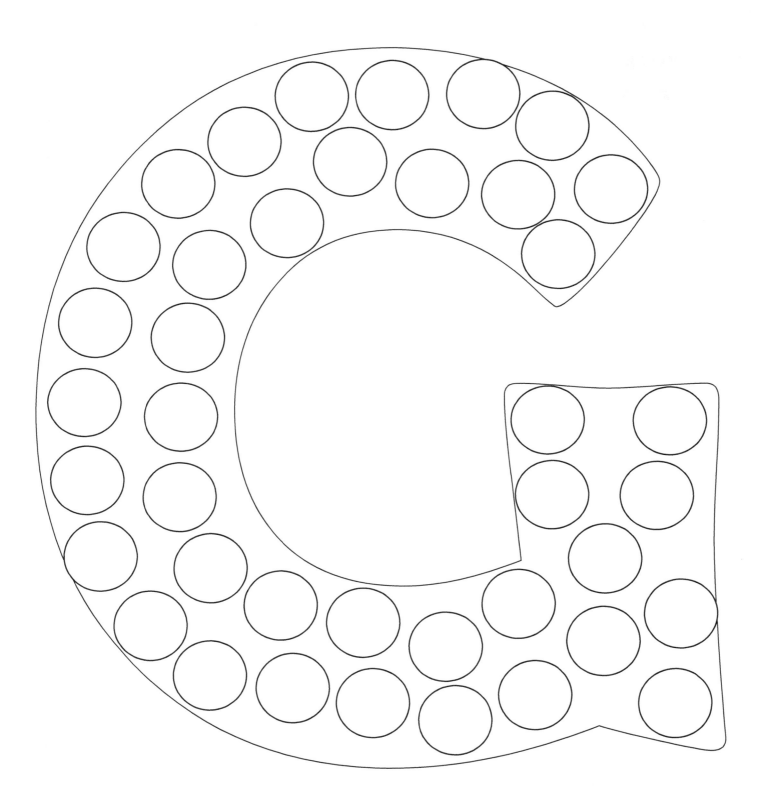

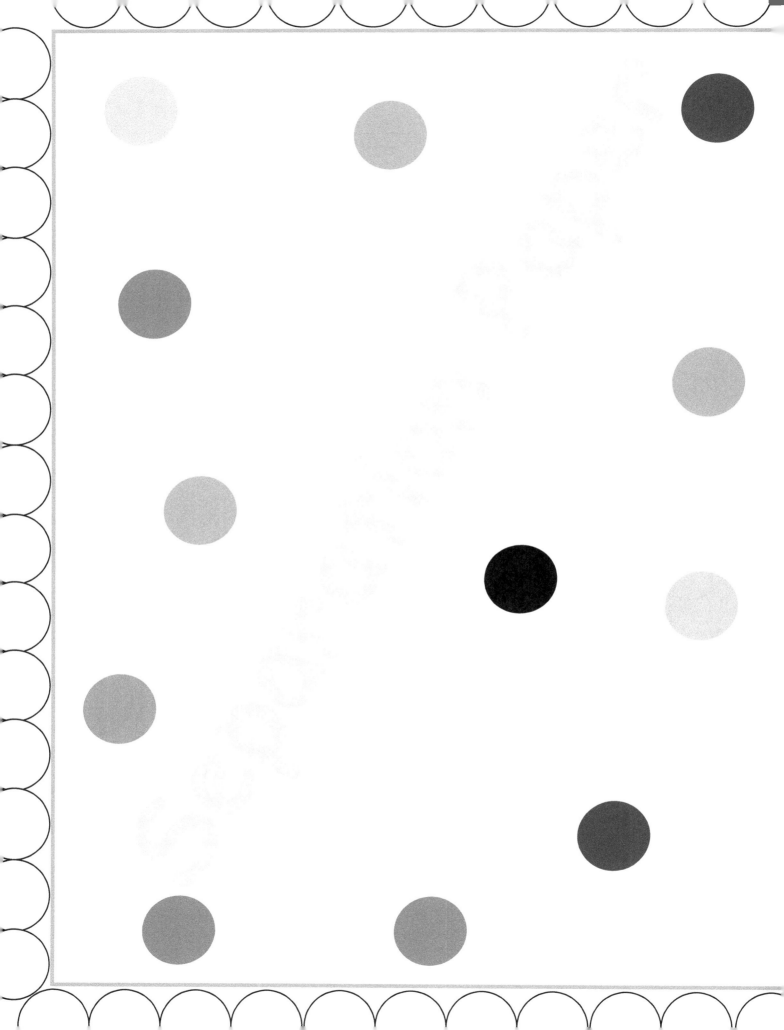

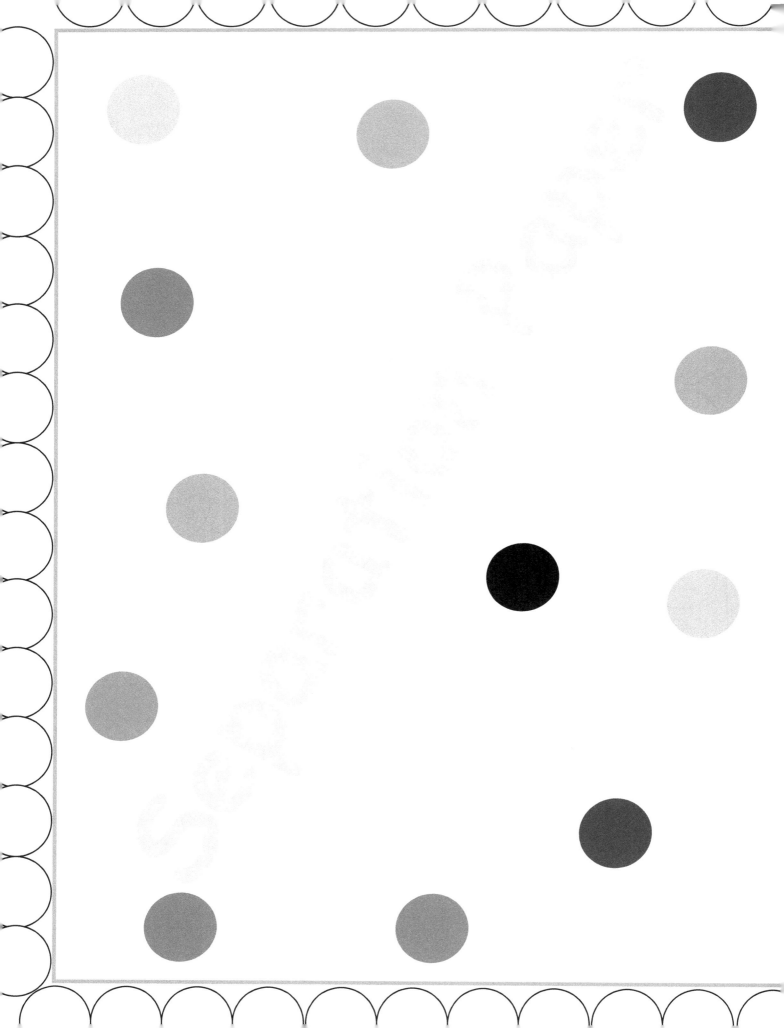

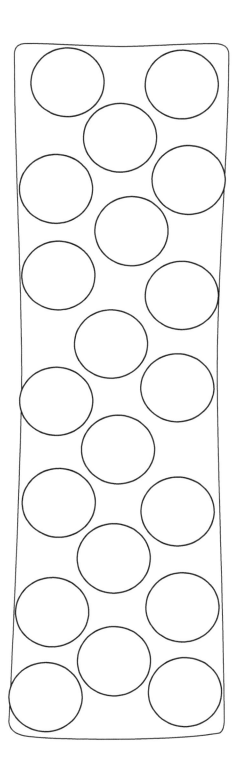

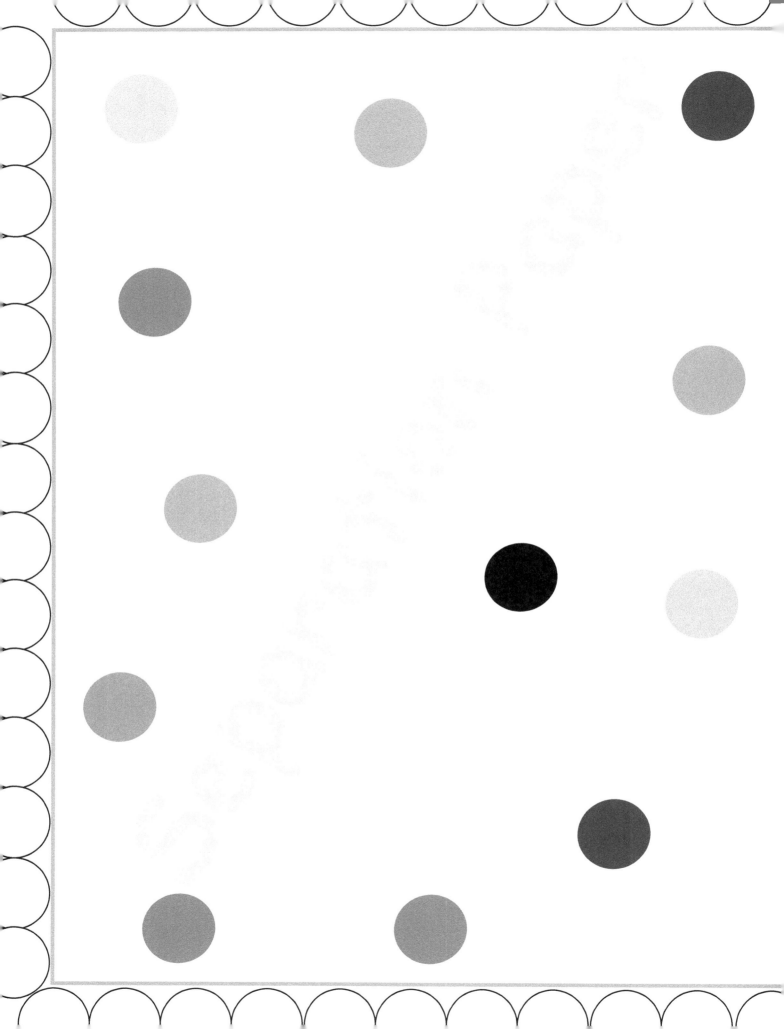

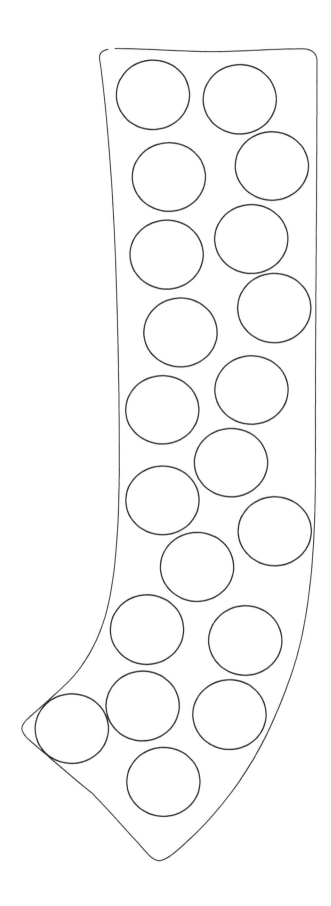

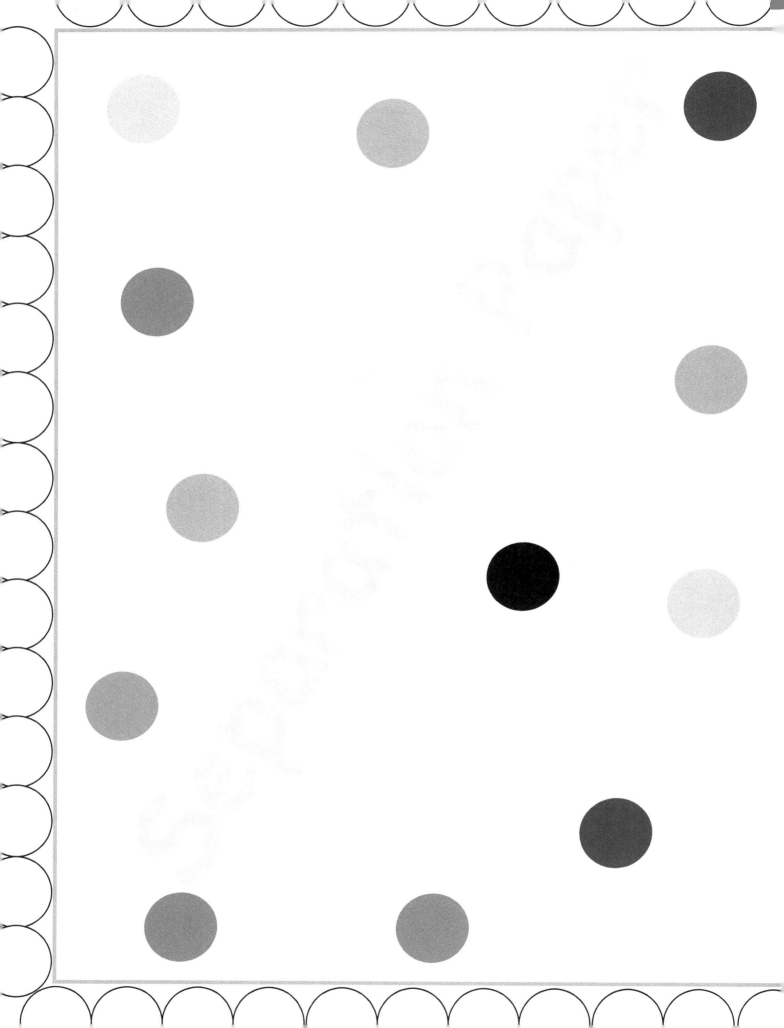

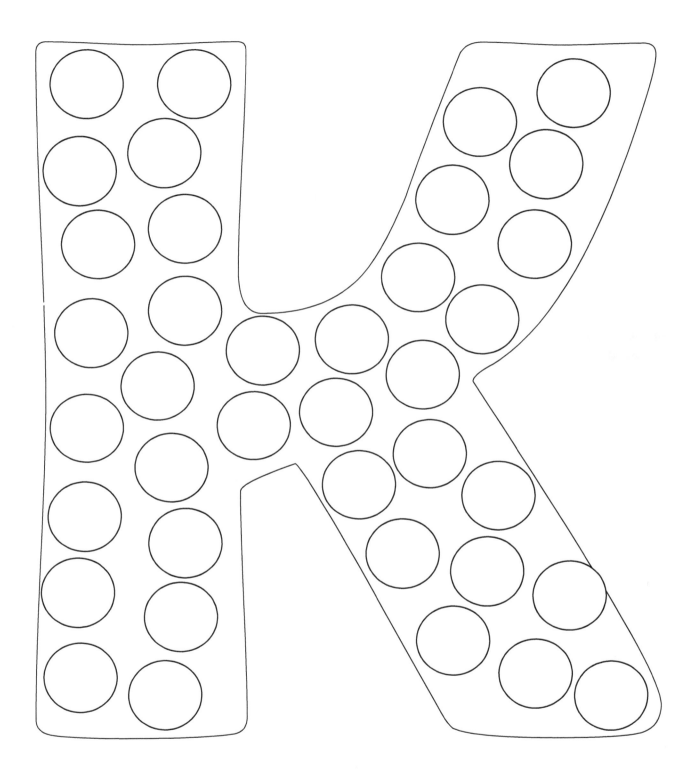

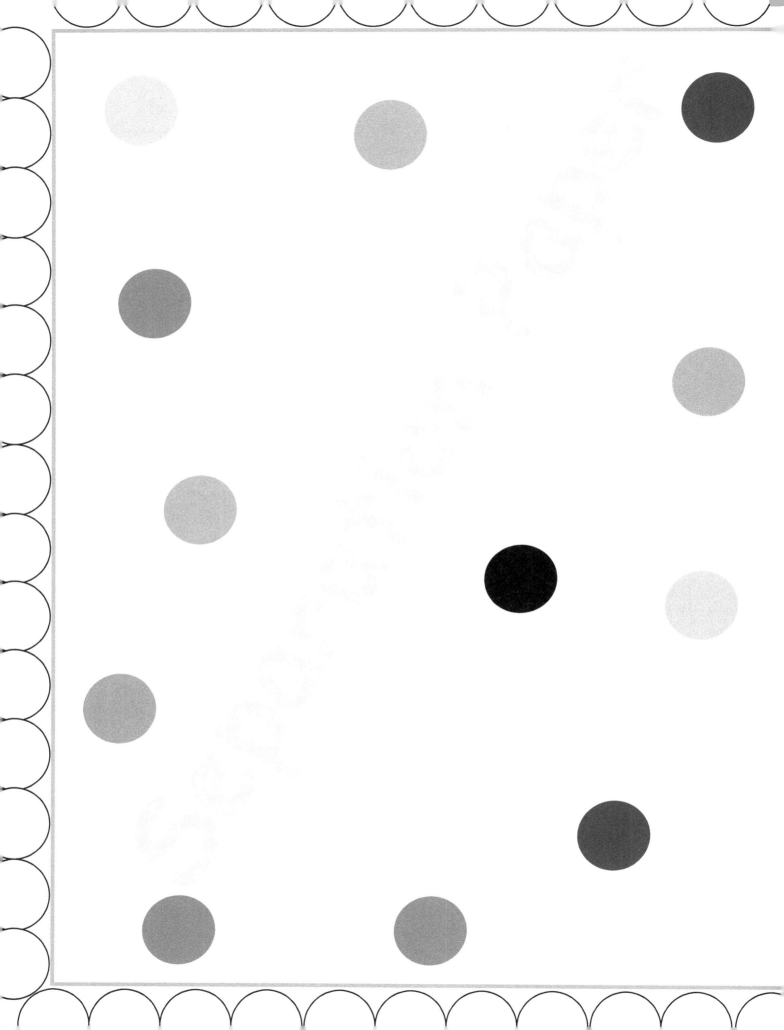

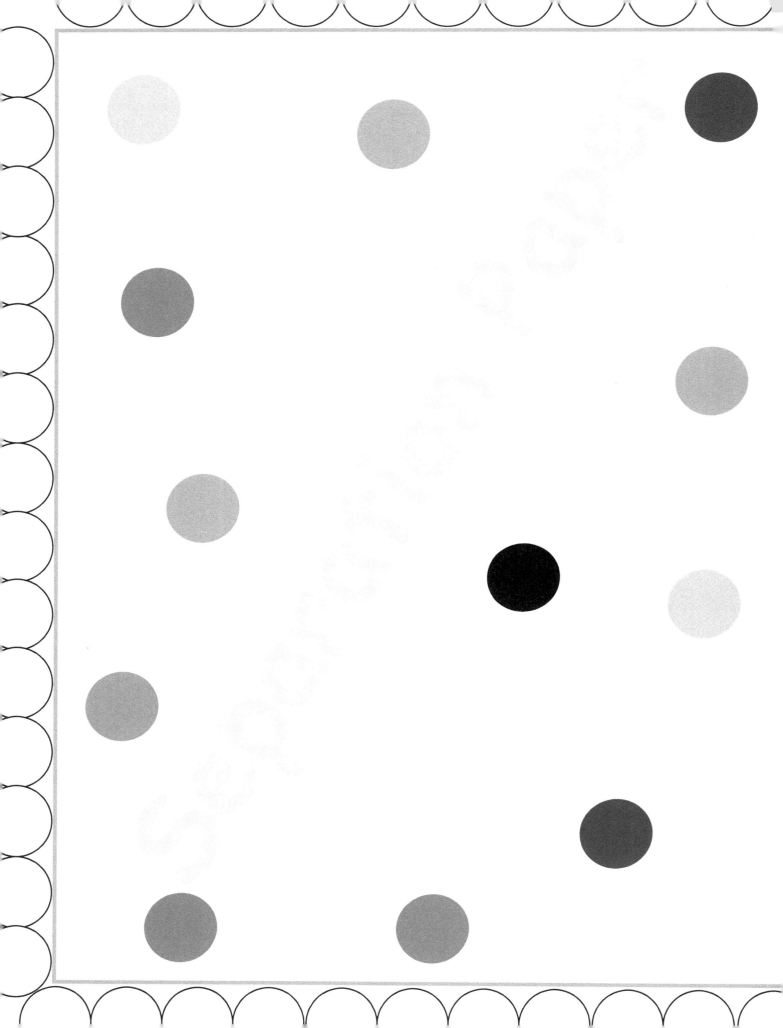

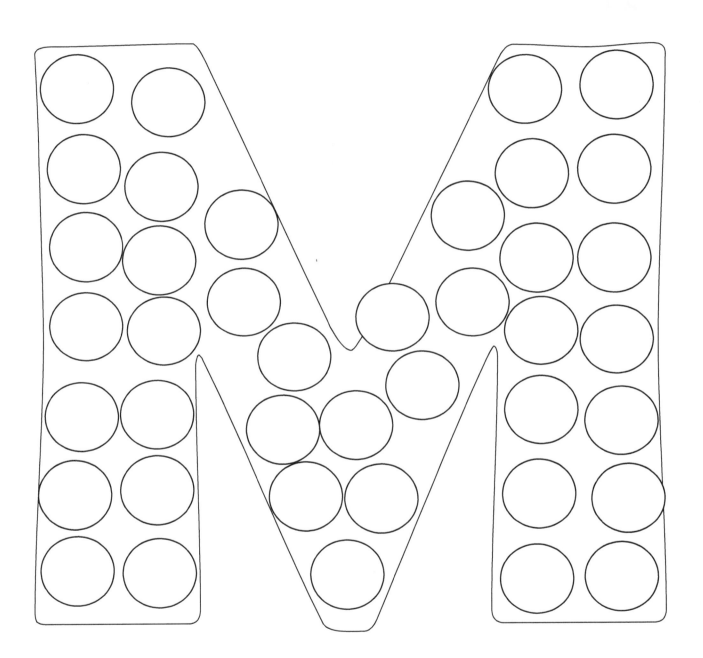

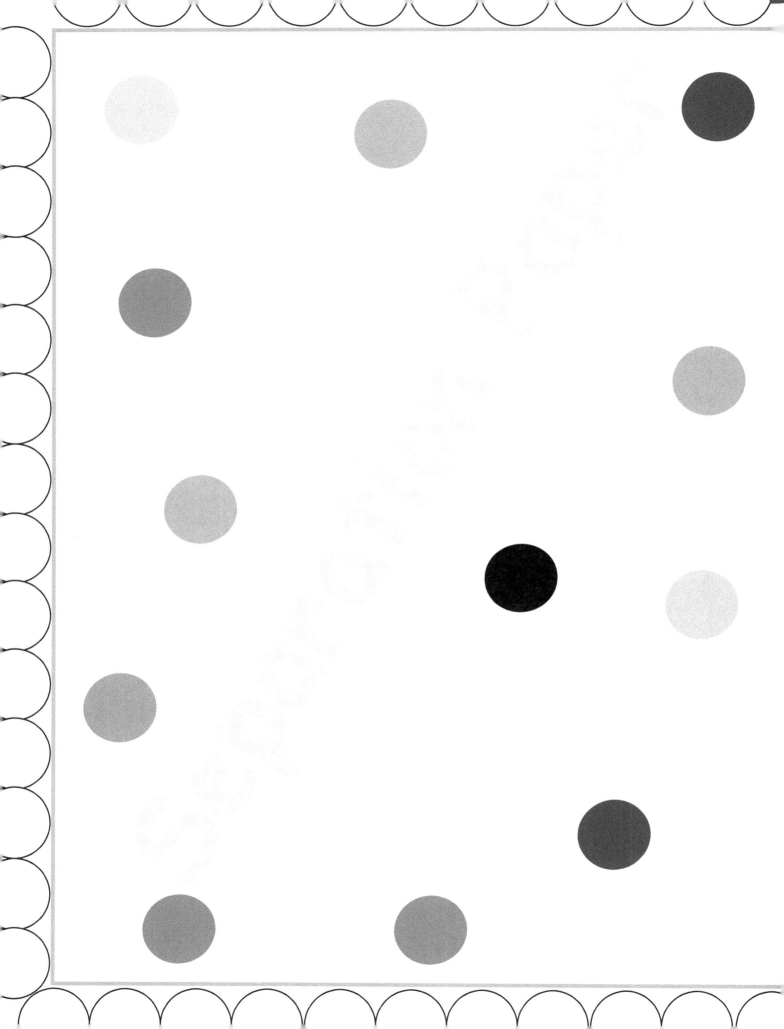

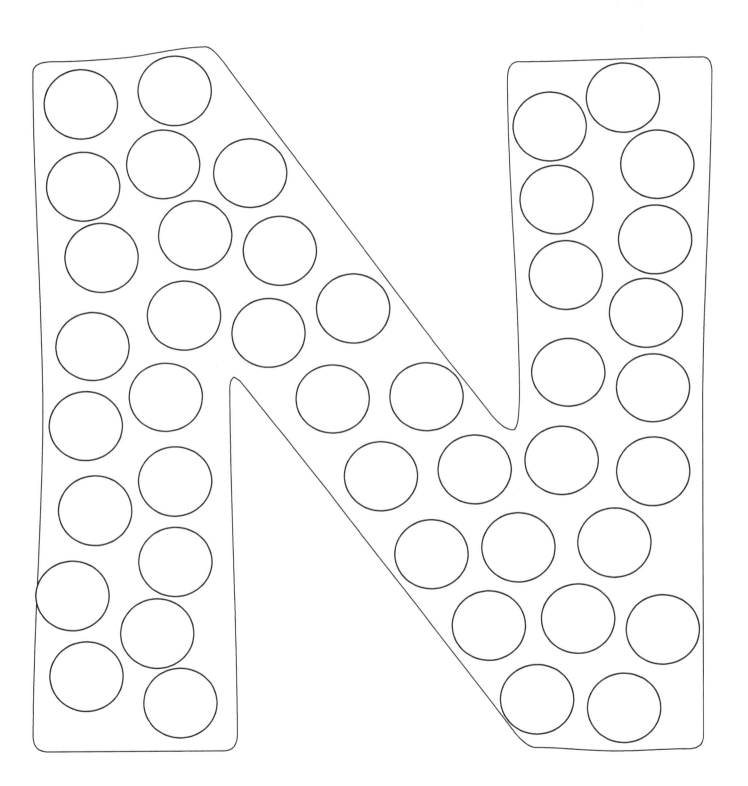

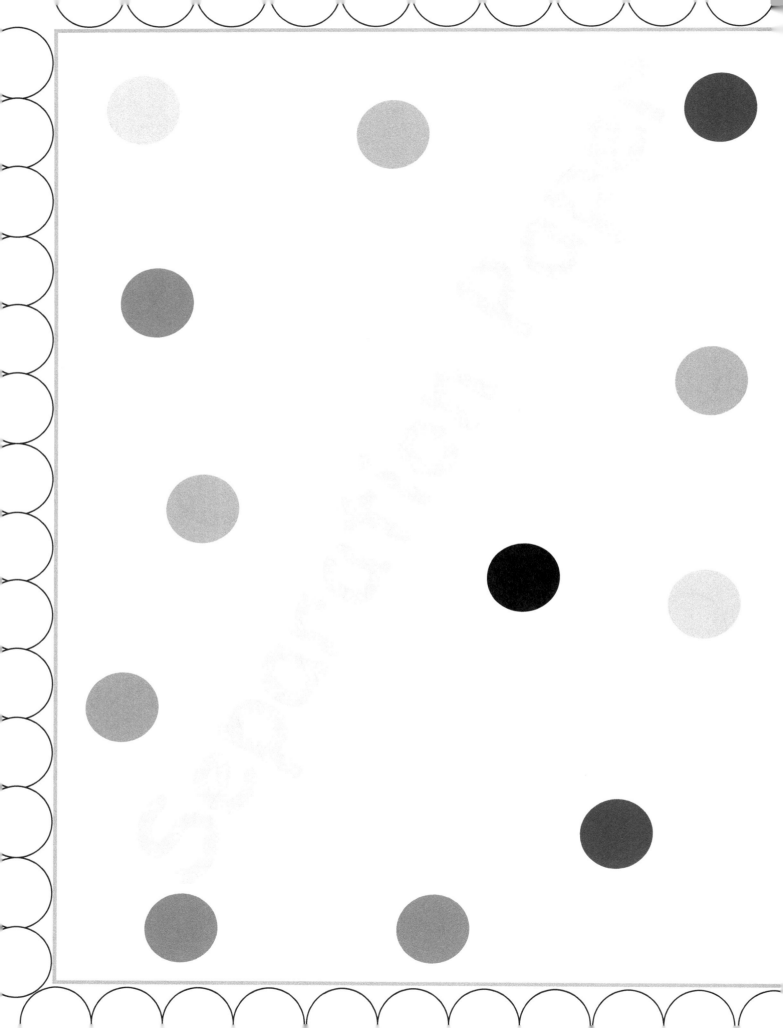

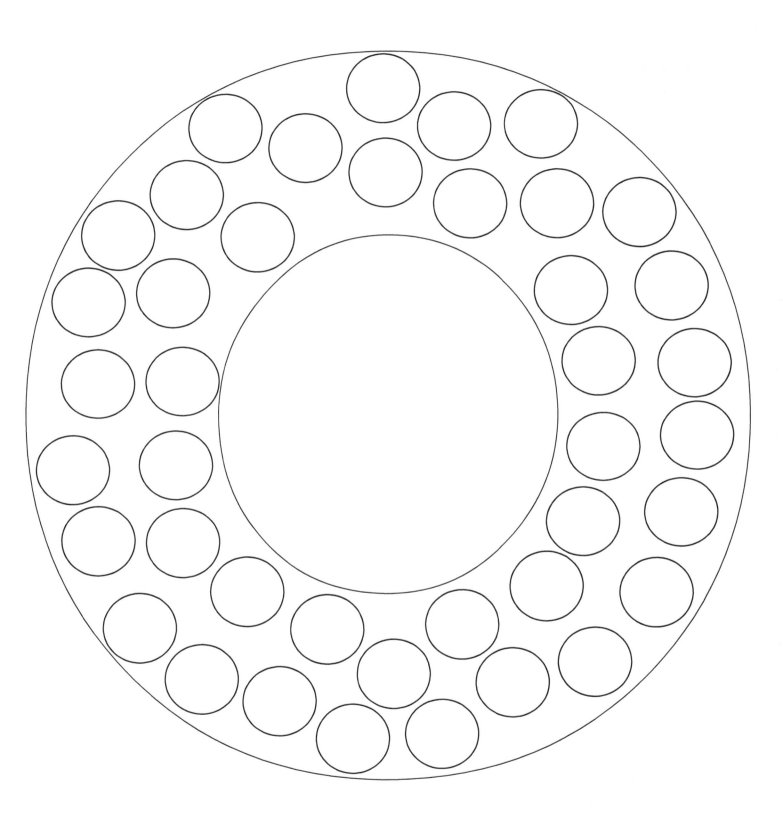

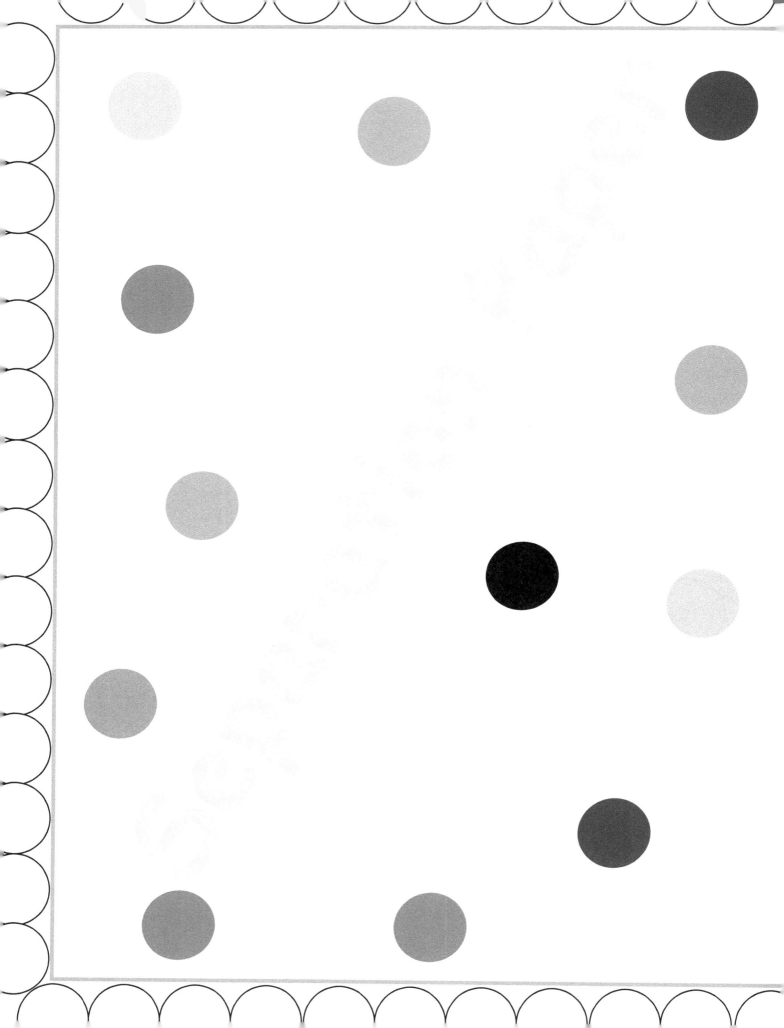

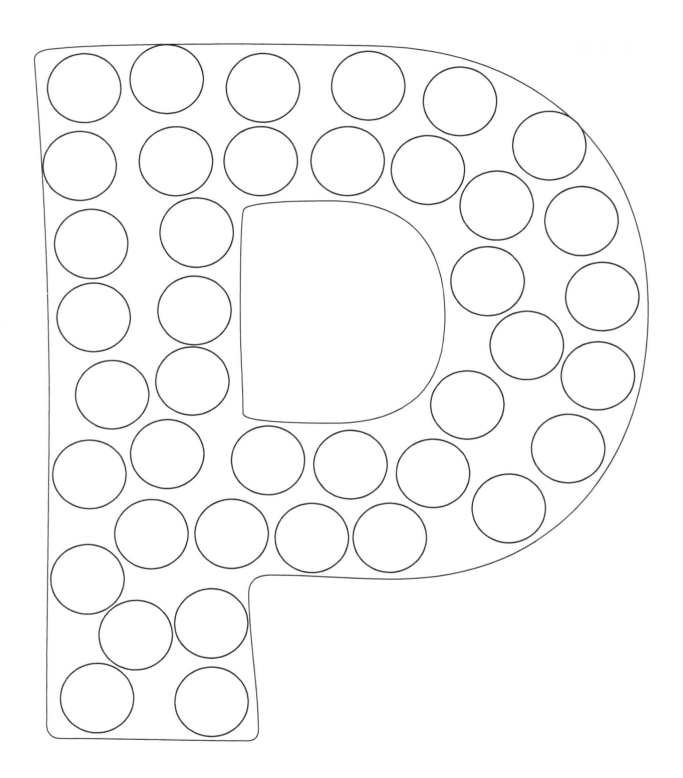

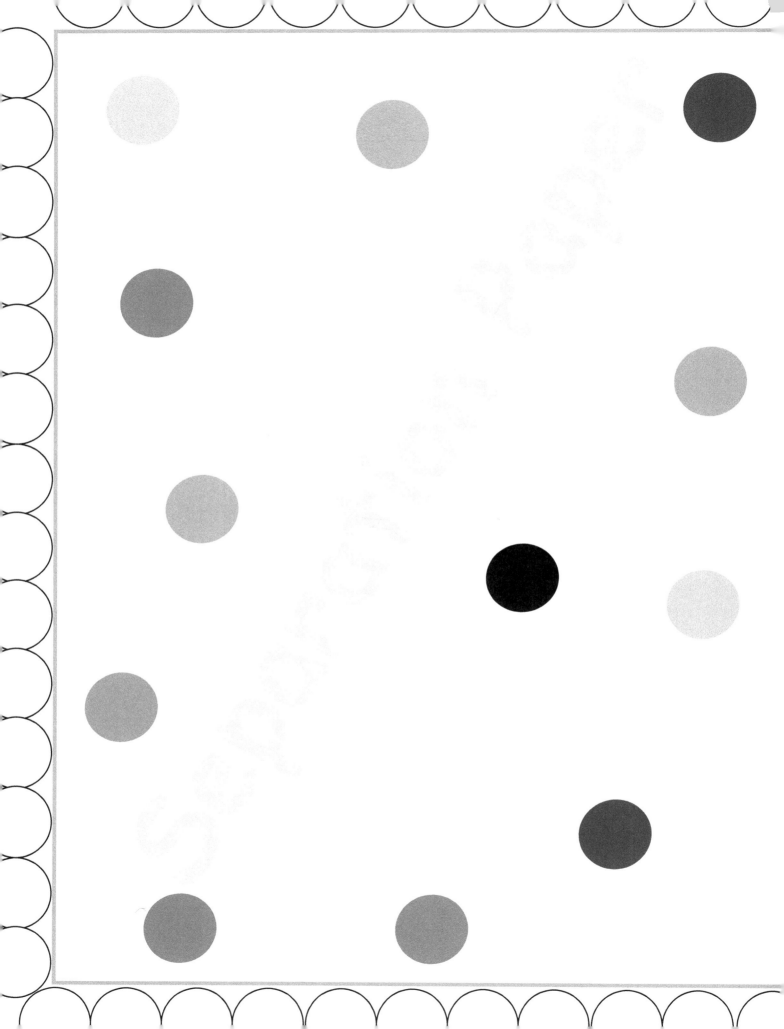

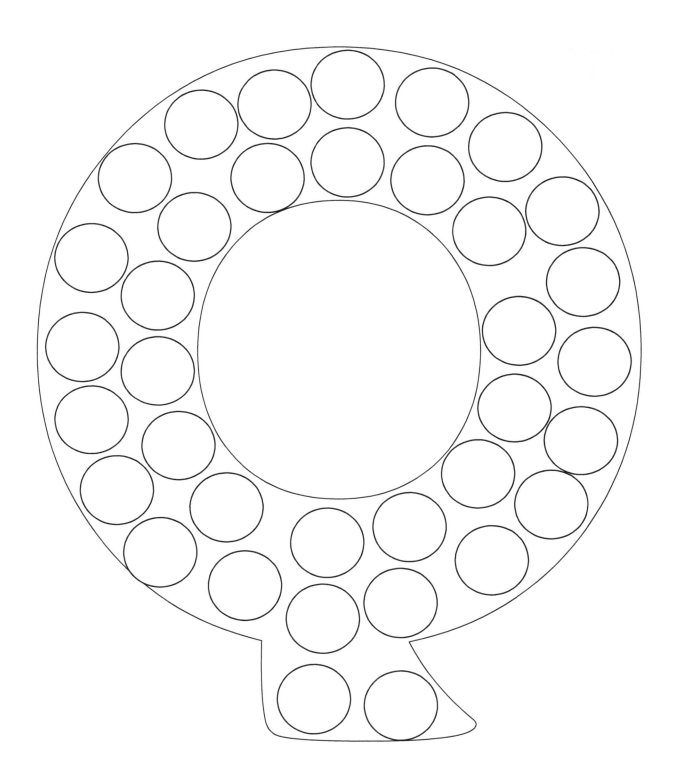

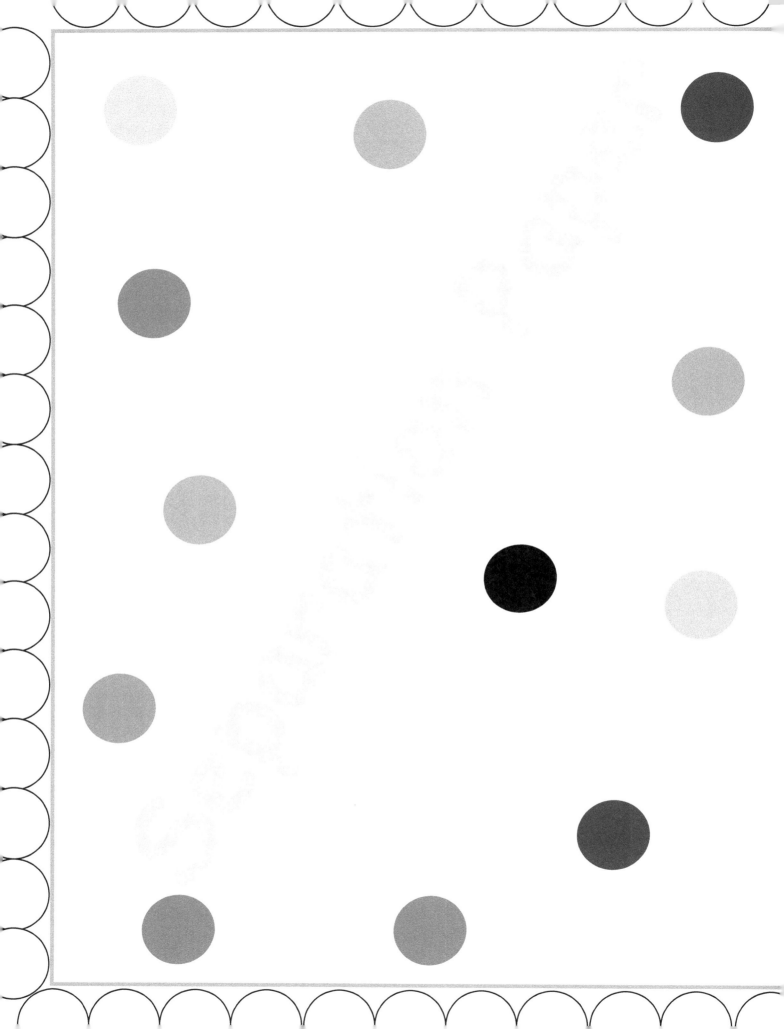

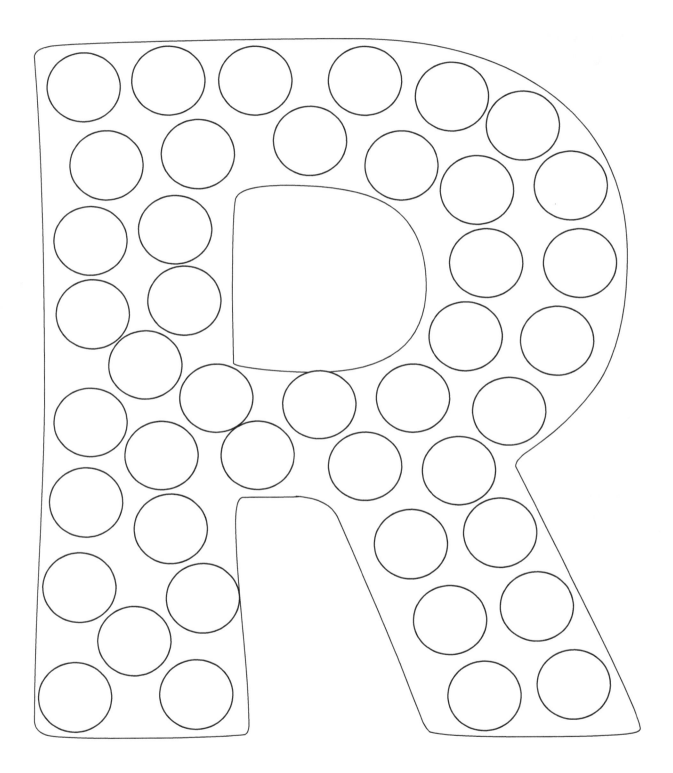

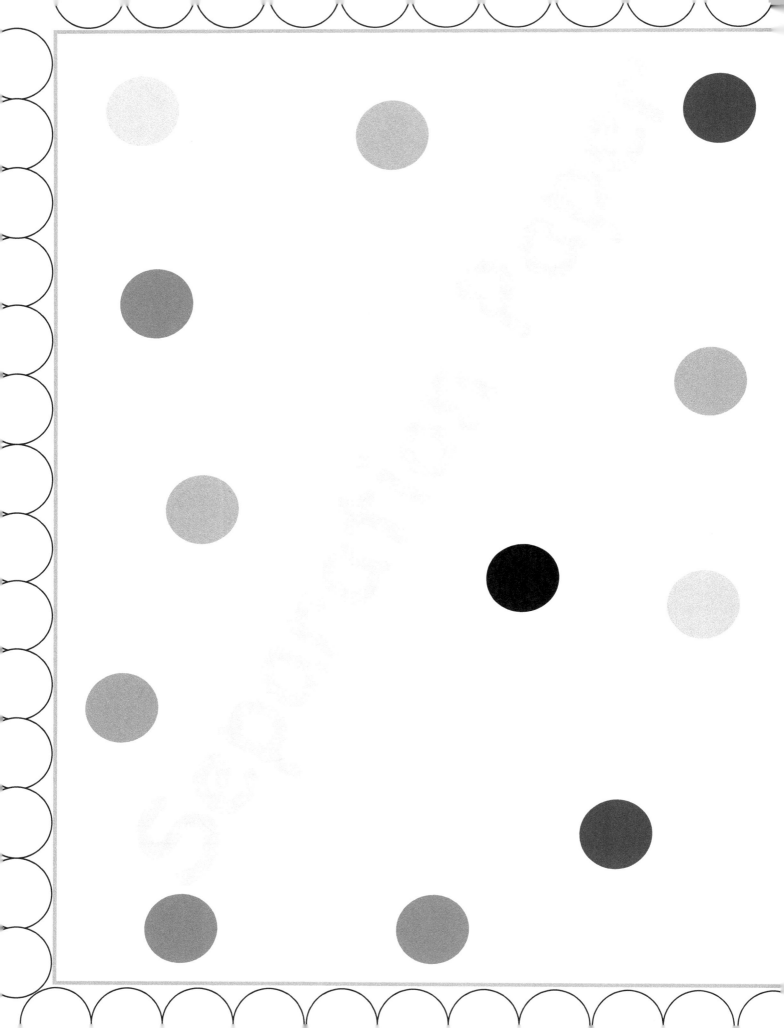

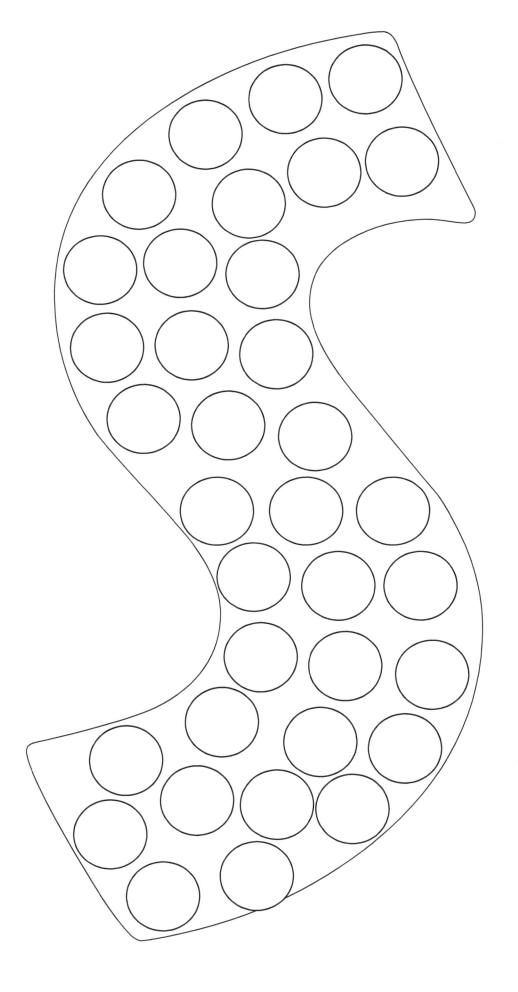

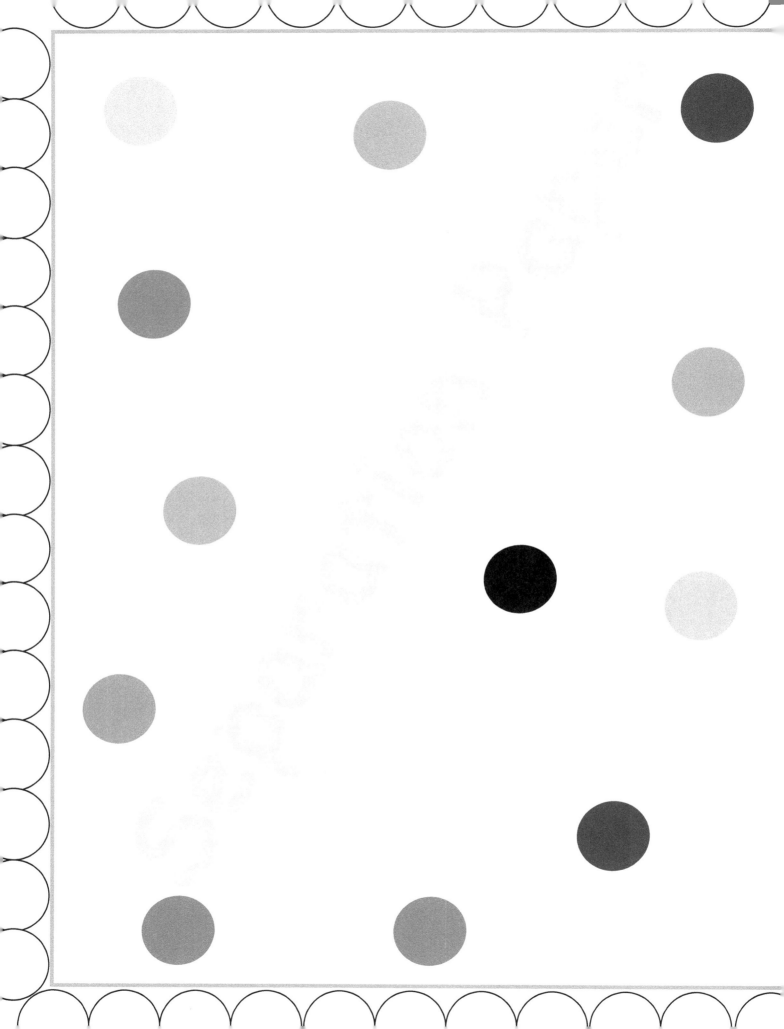

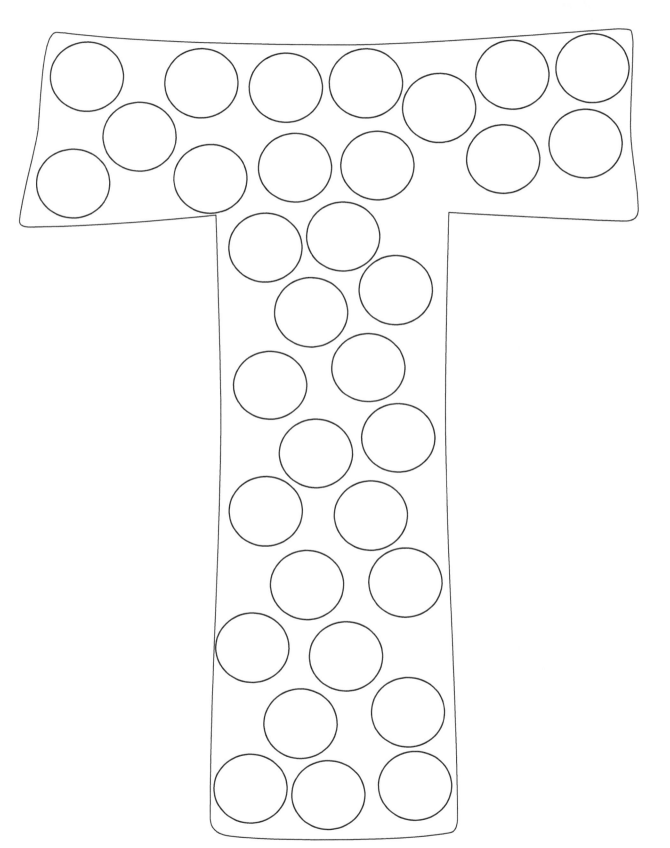

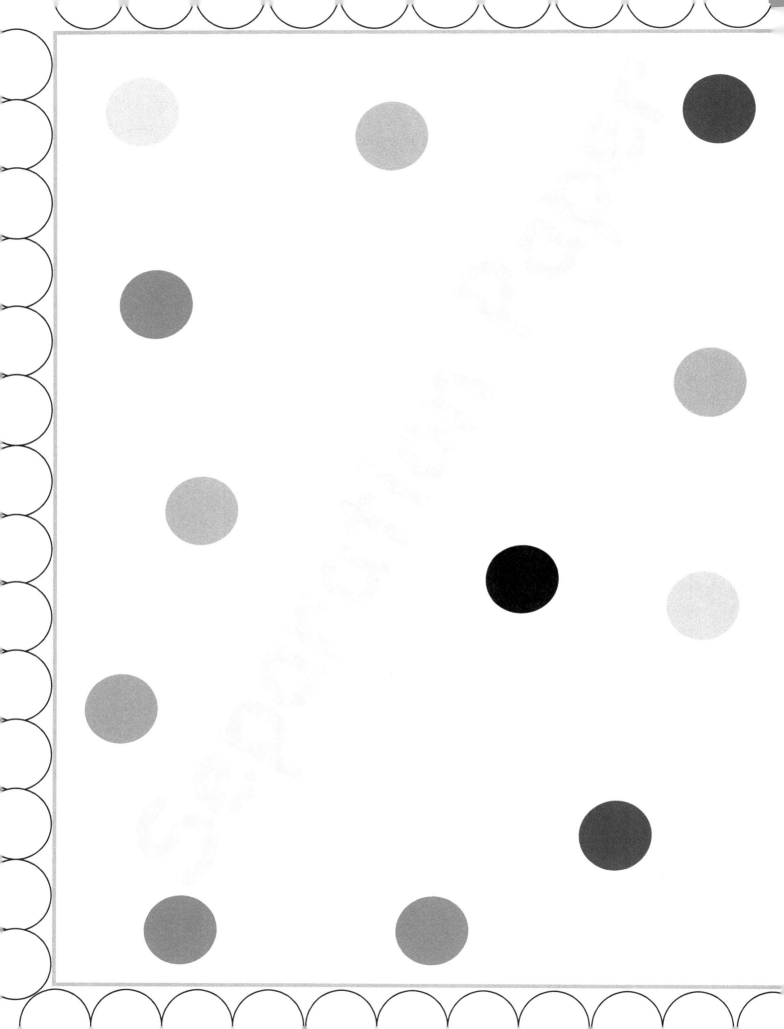

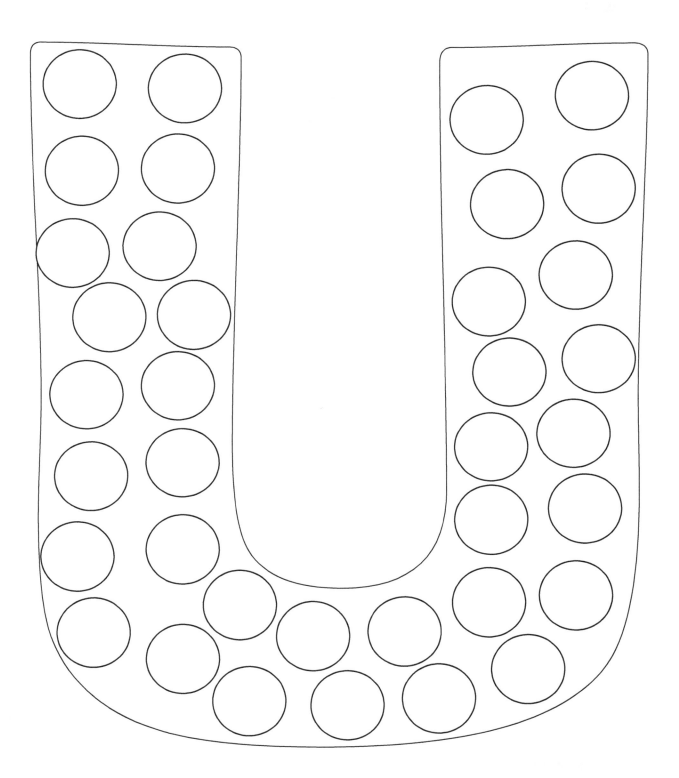

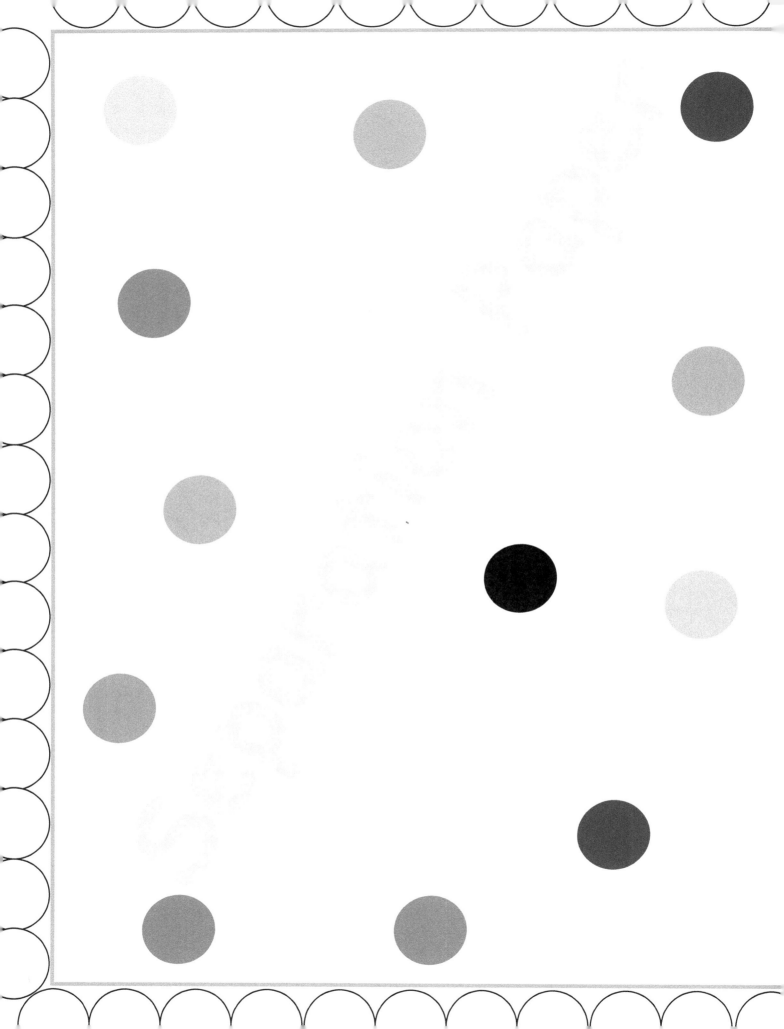

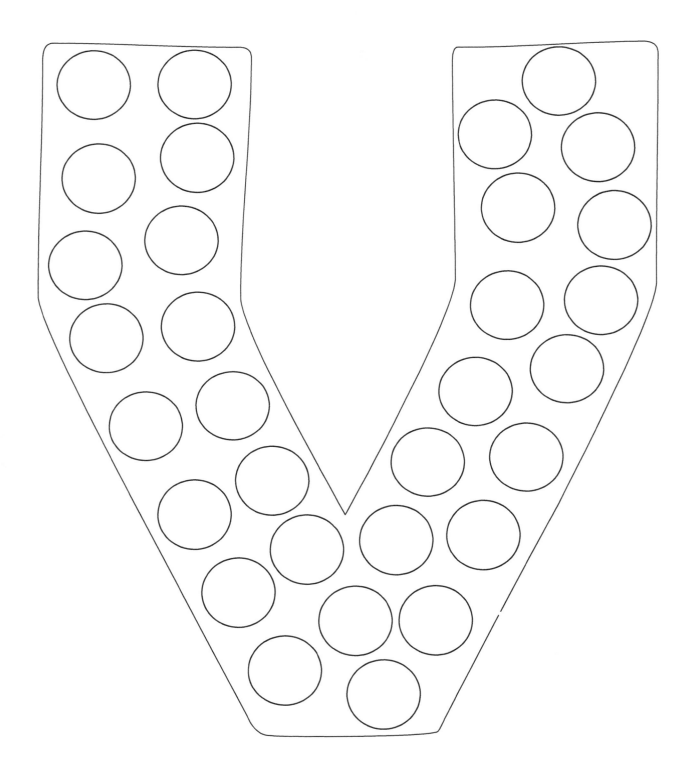

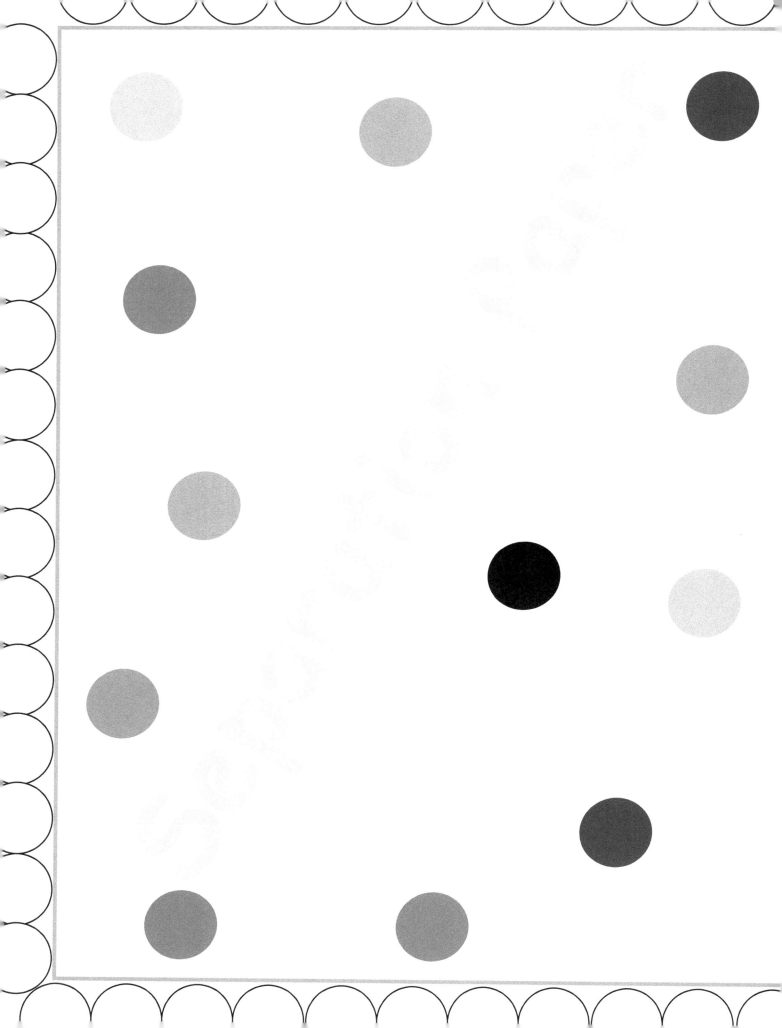

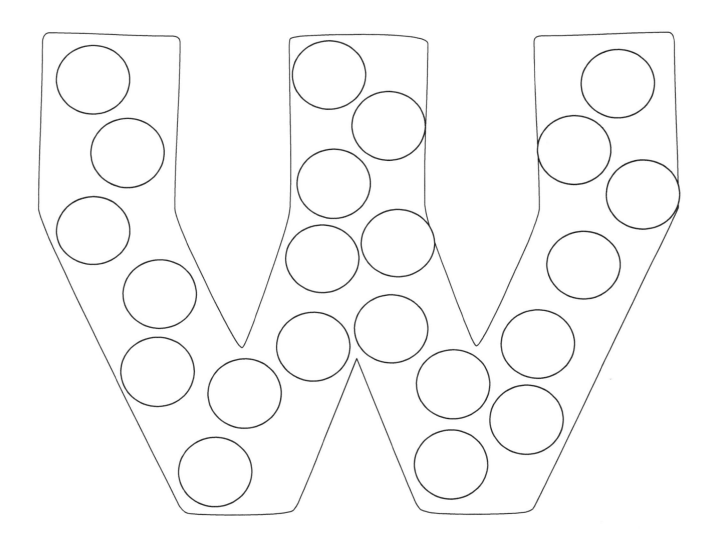

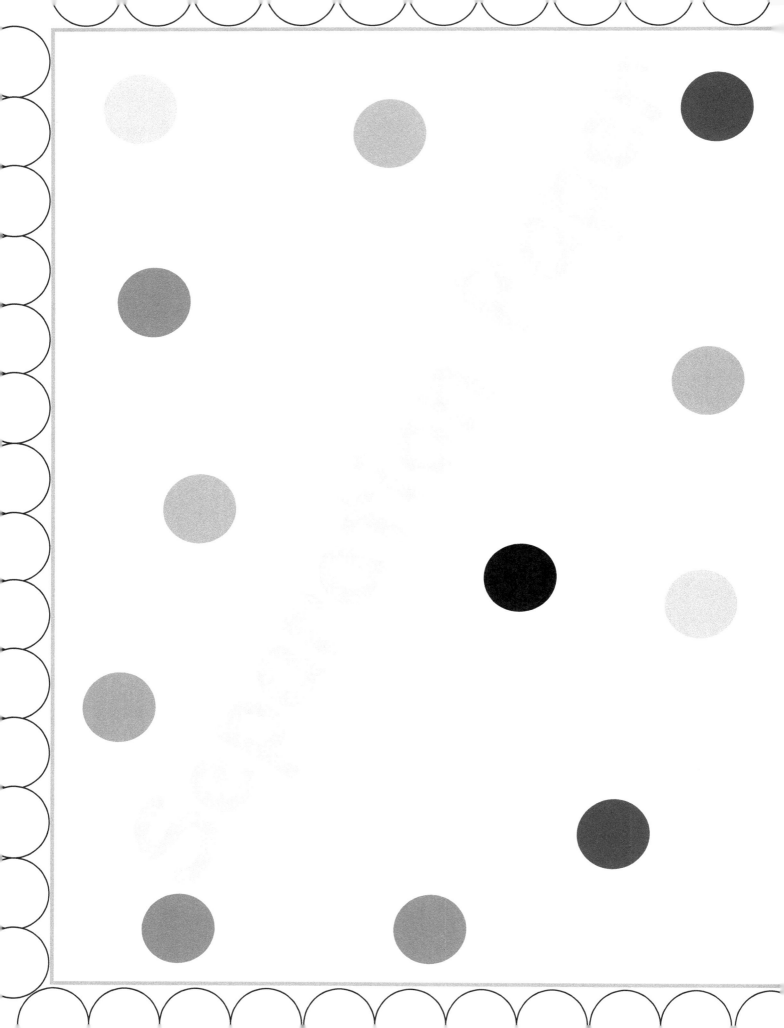

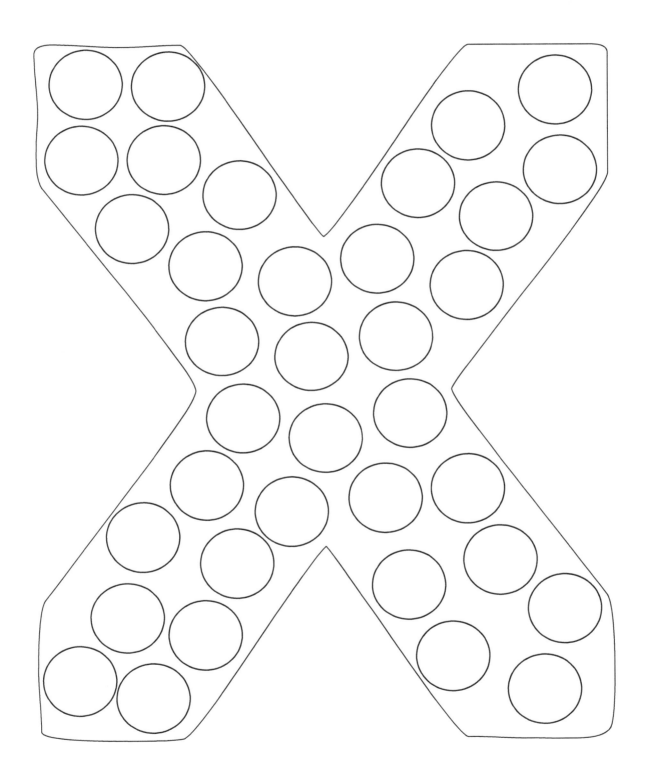

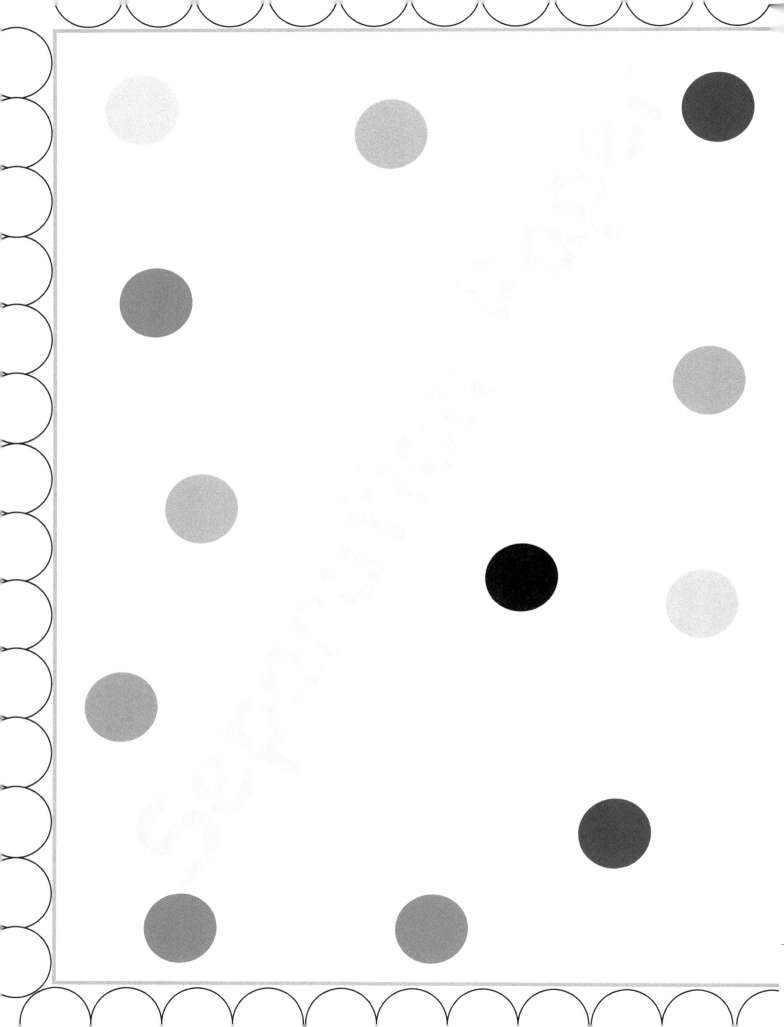

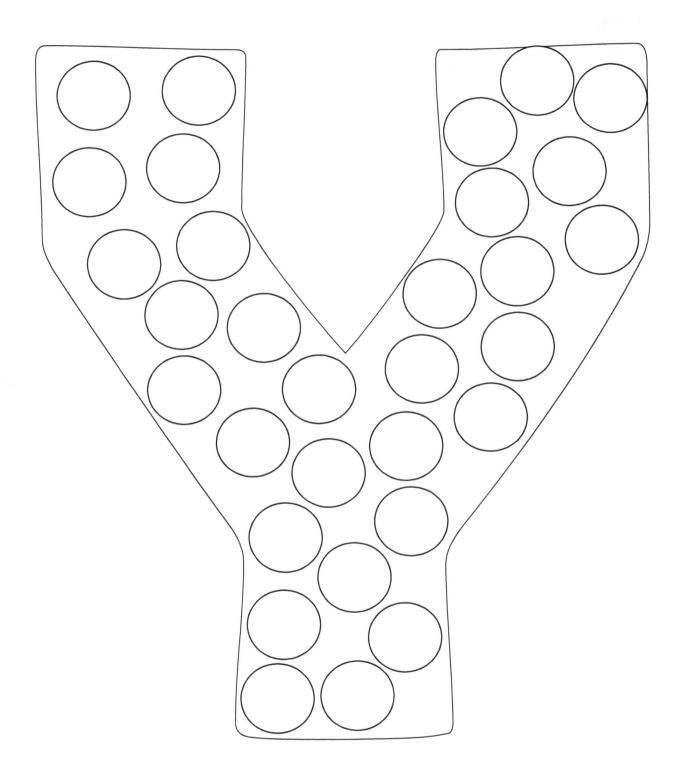

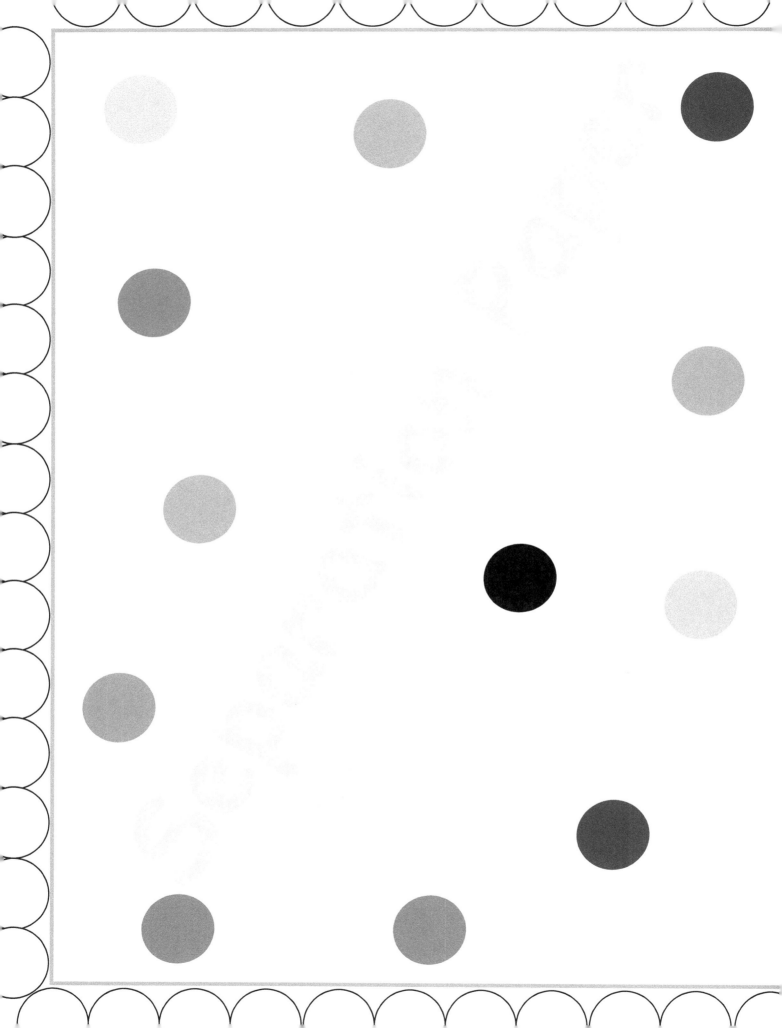

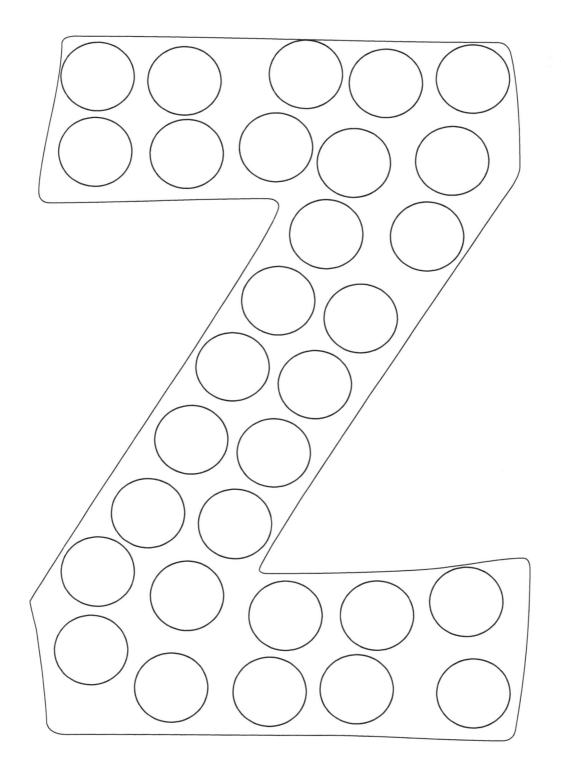

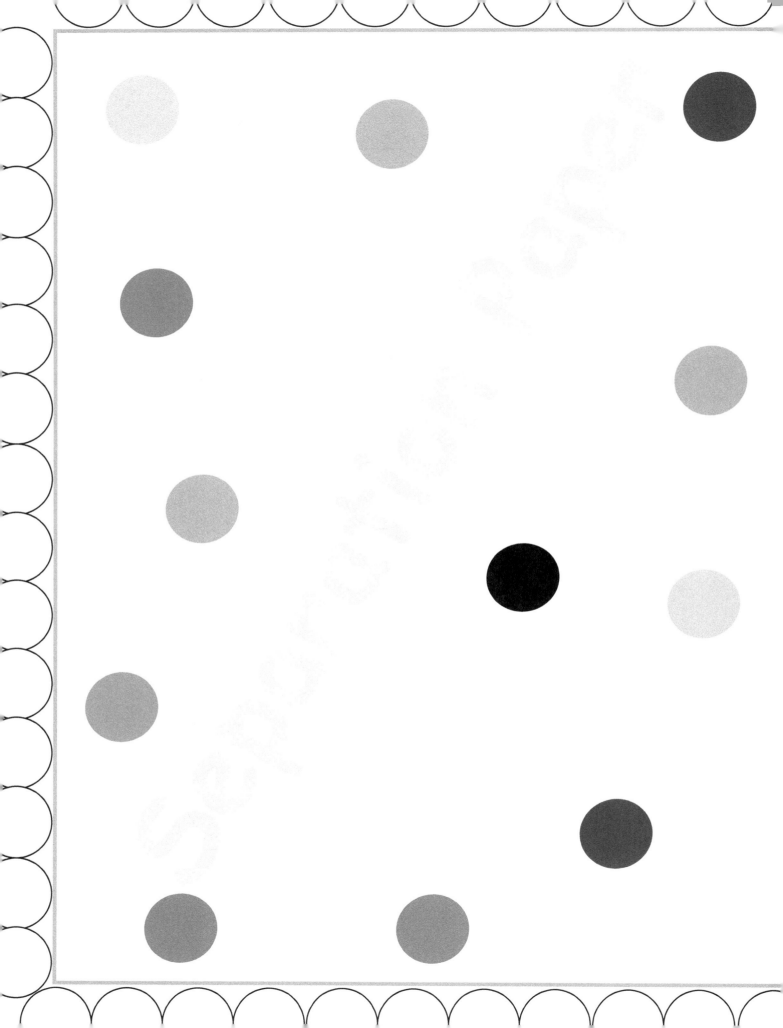

Color the Following Numbers

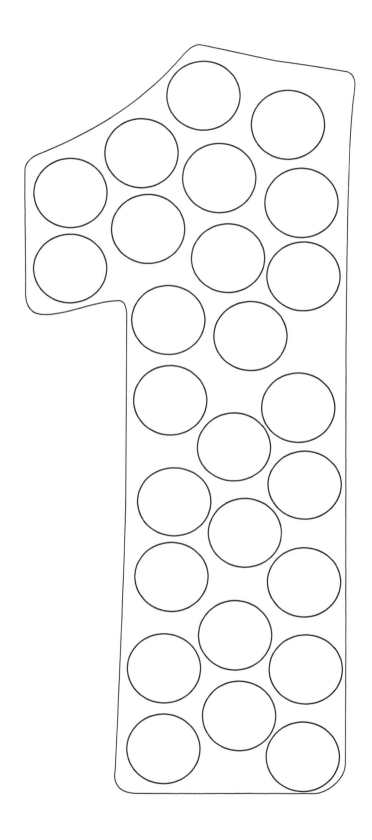

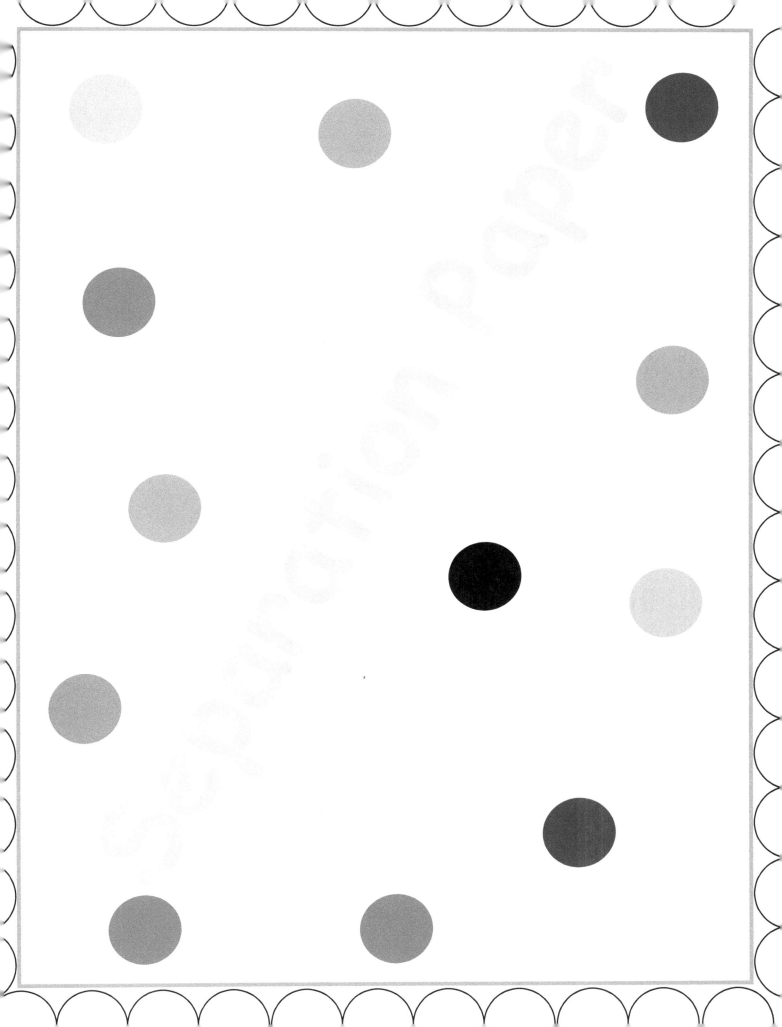

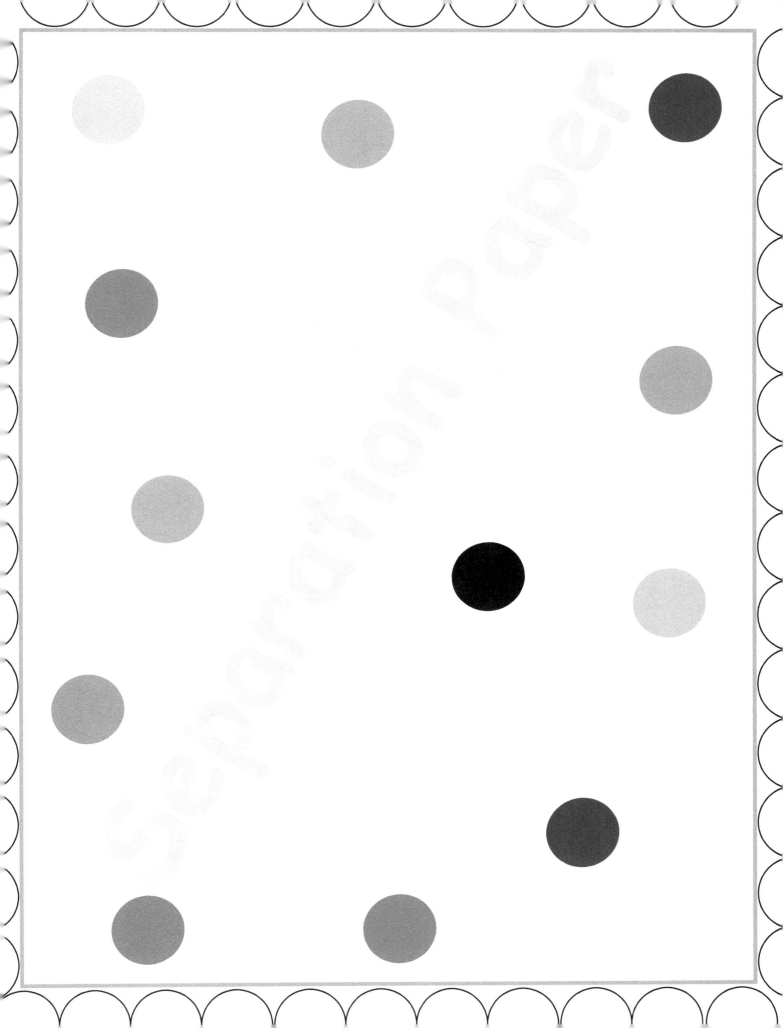

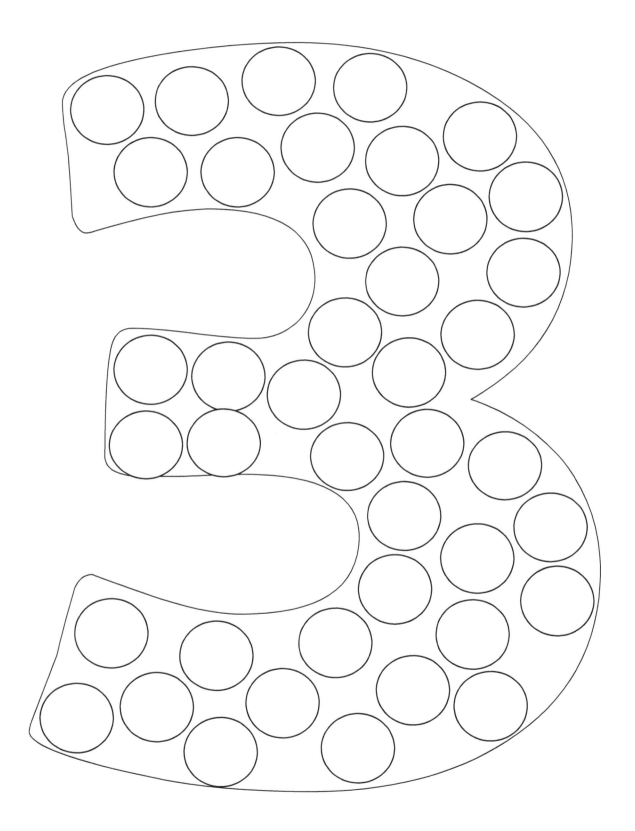

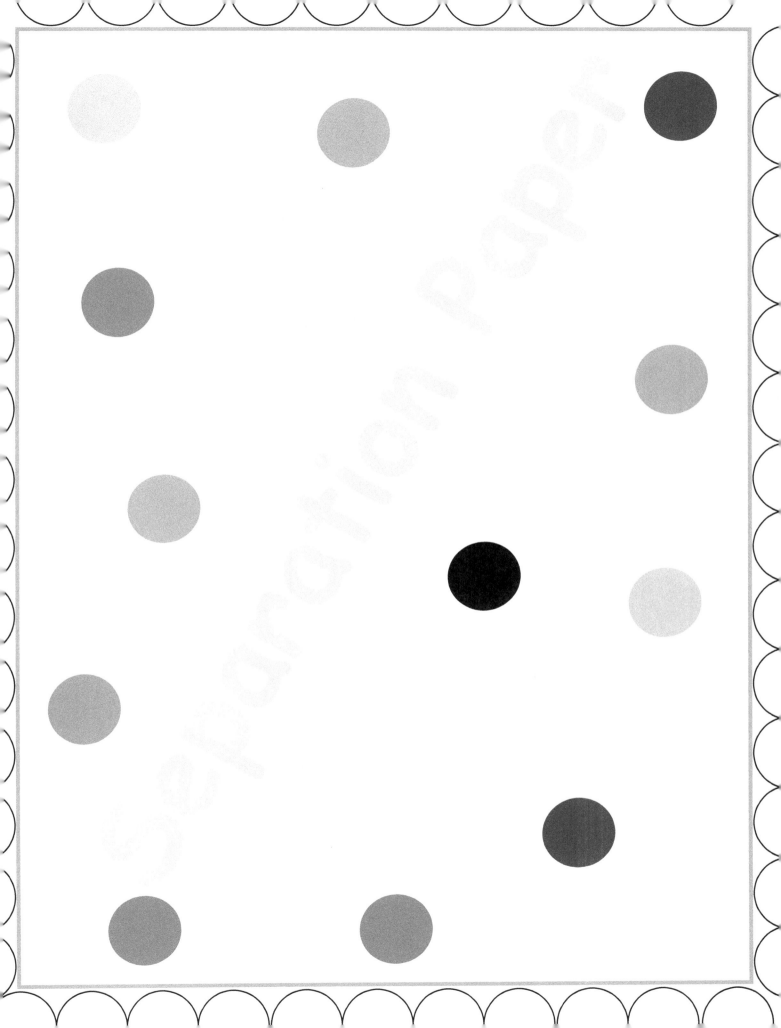

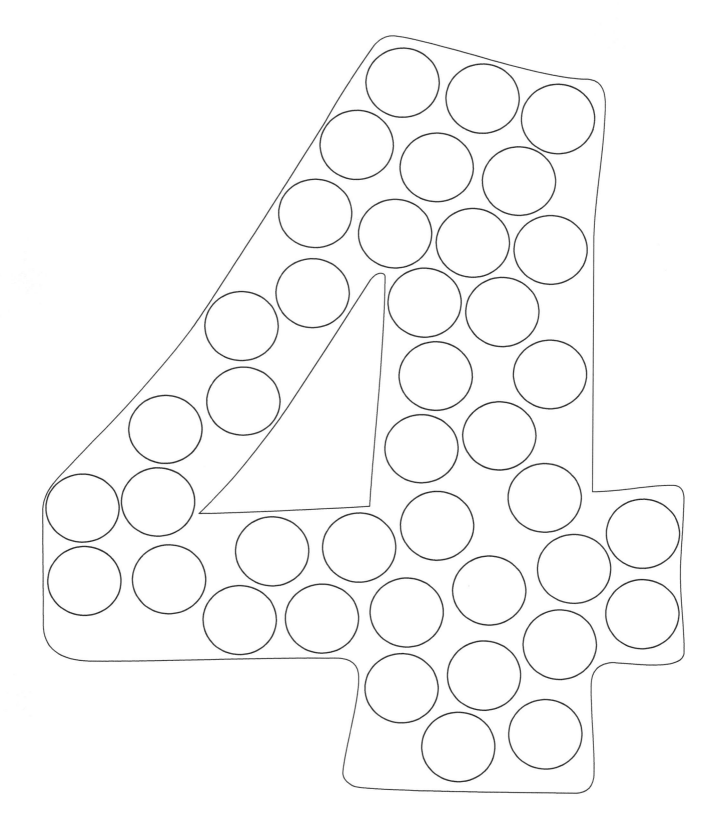

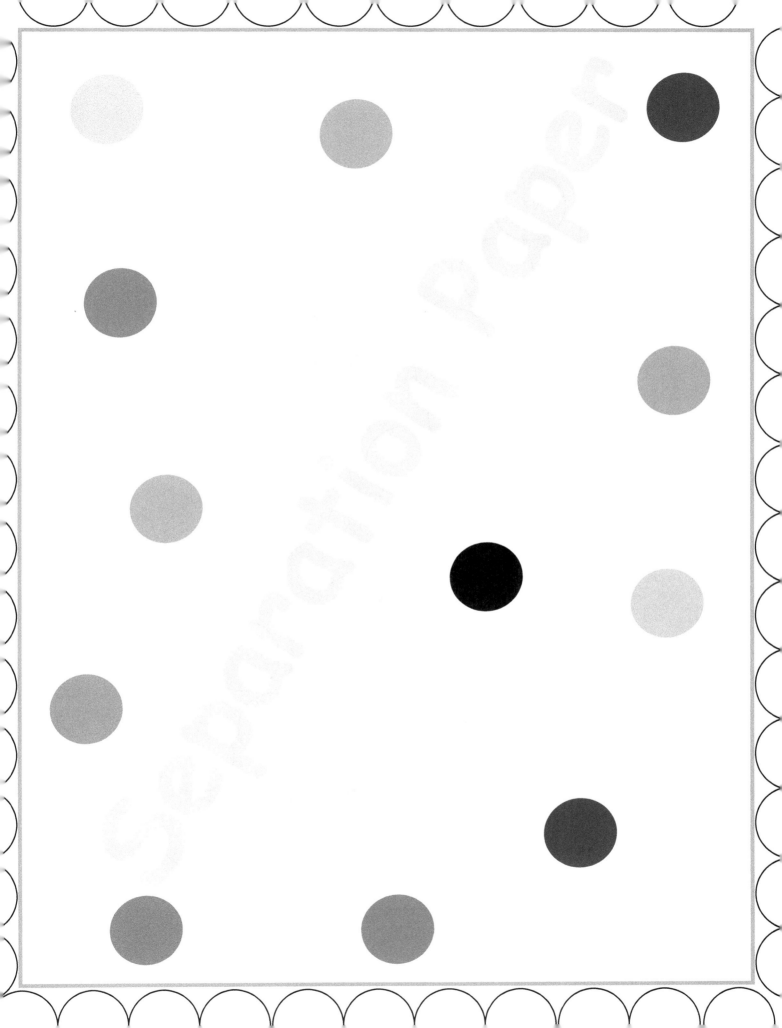

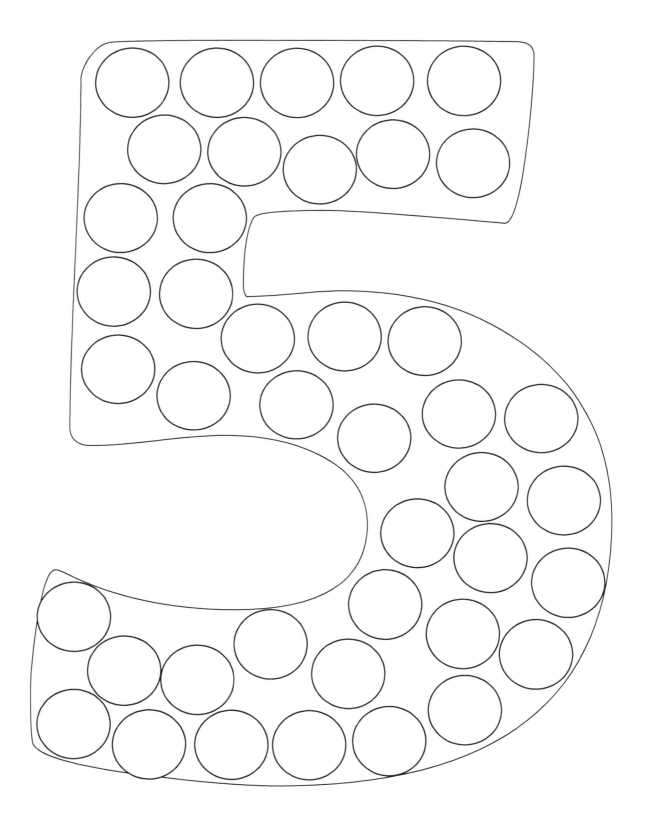

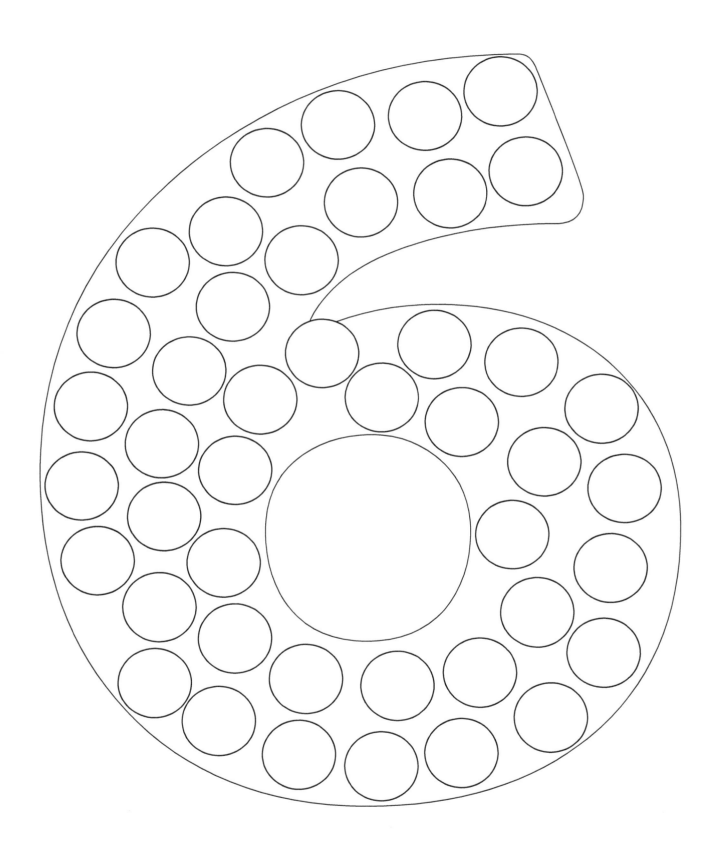

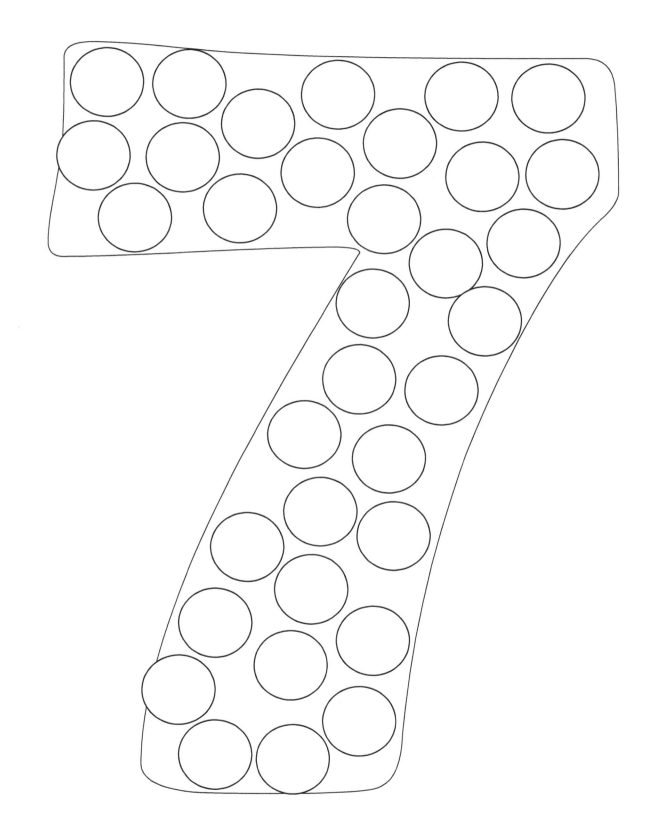

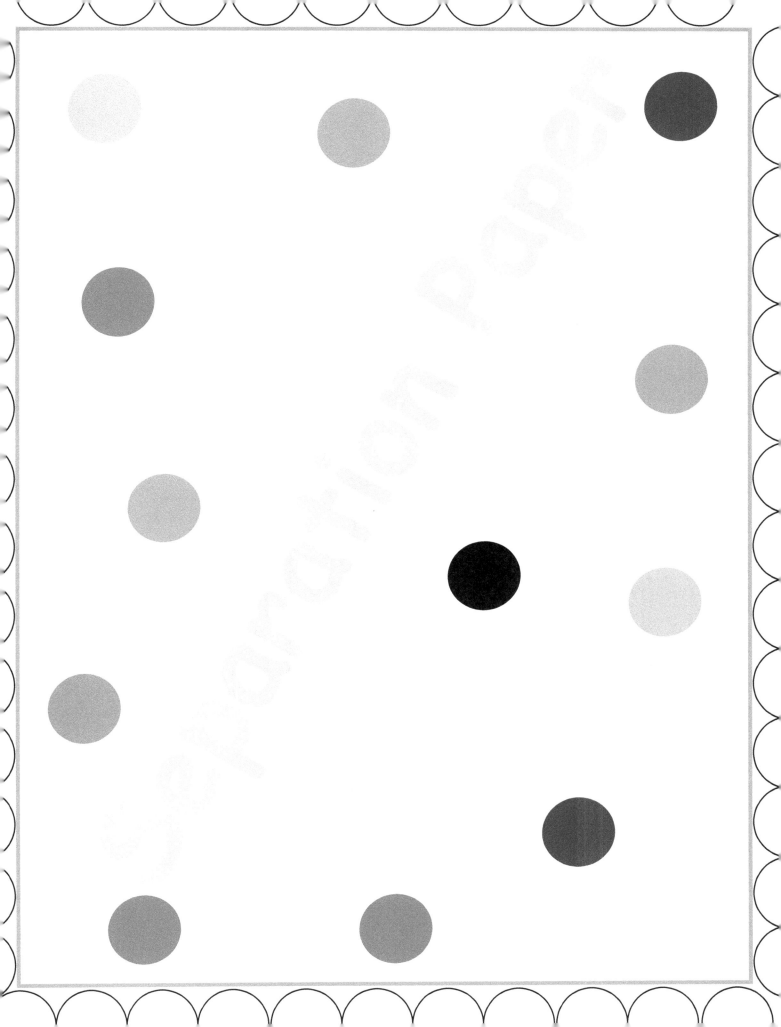

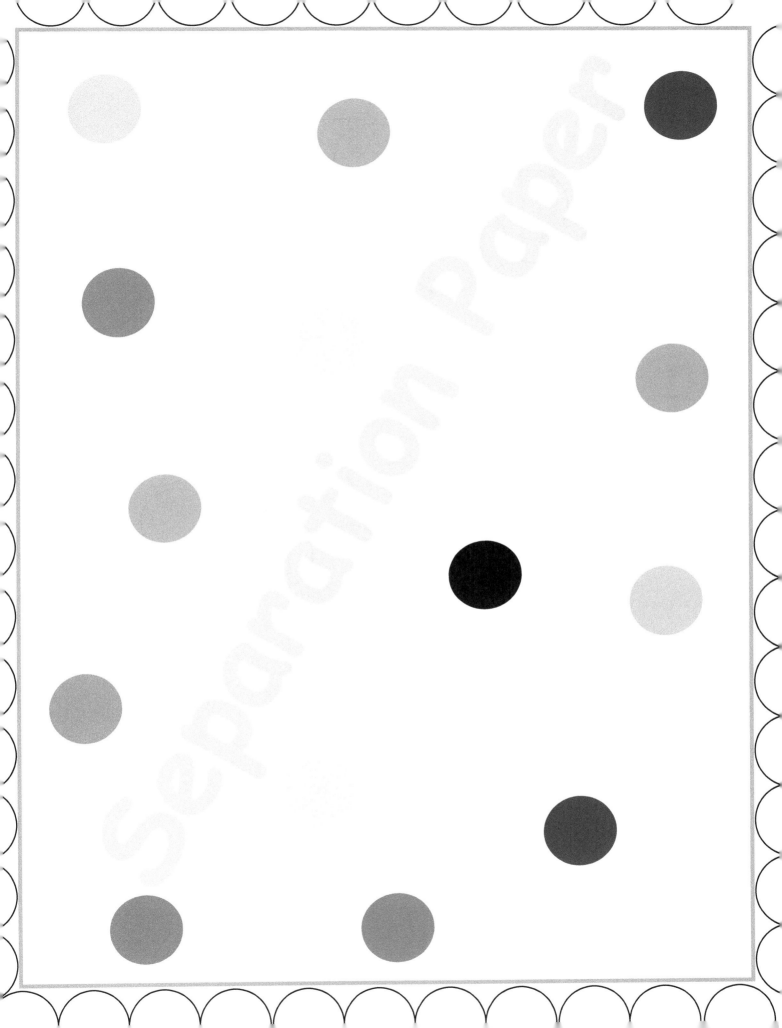

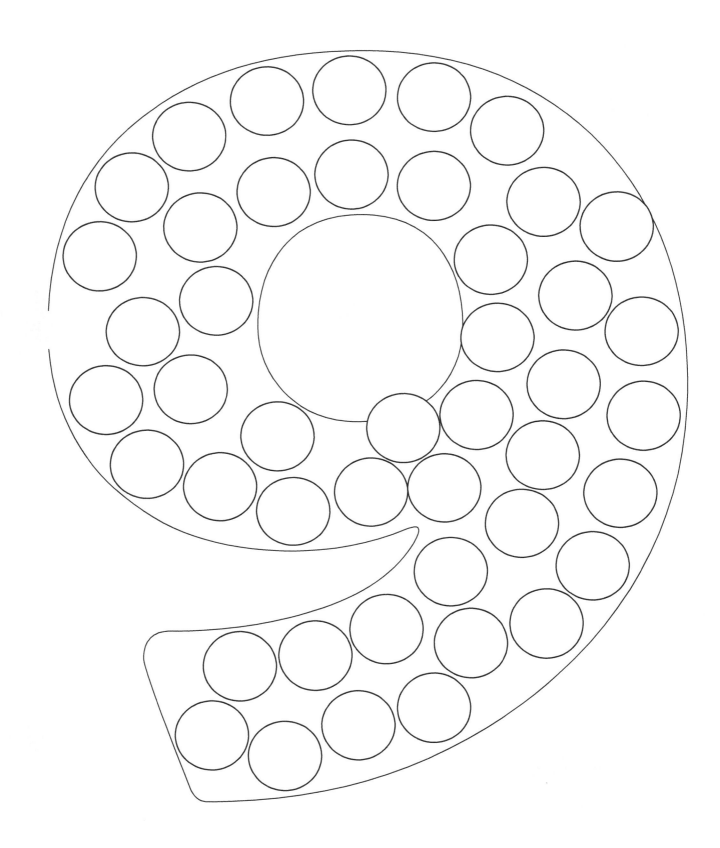

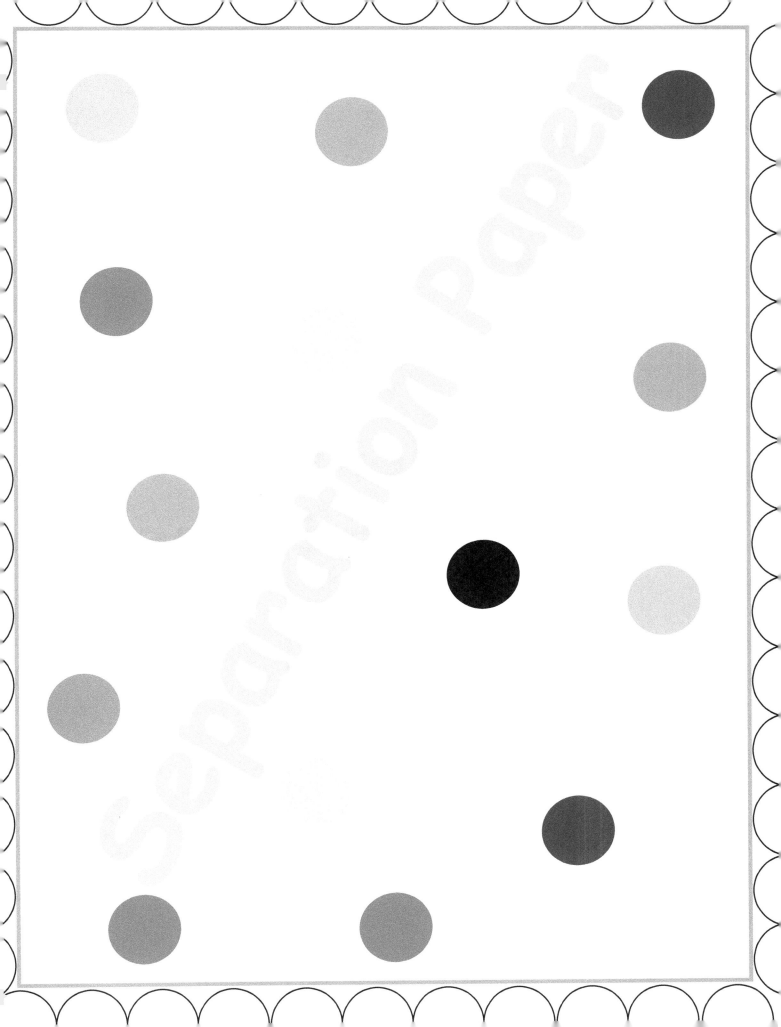

Color the following Shapes

Color the square

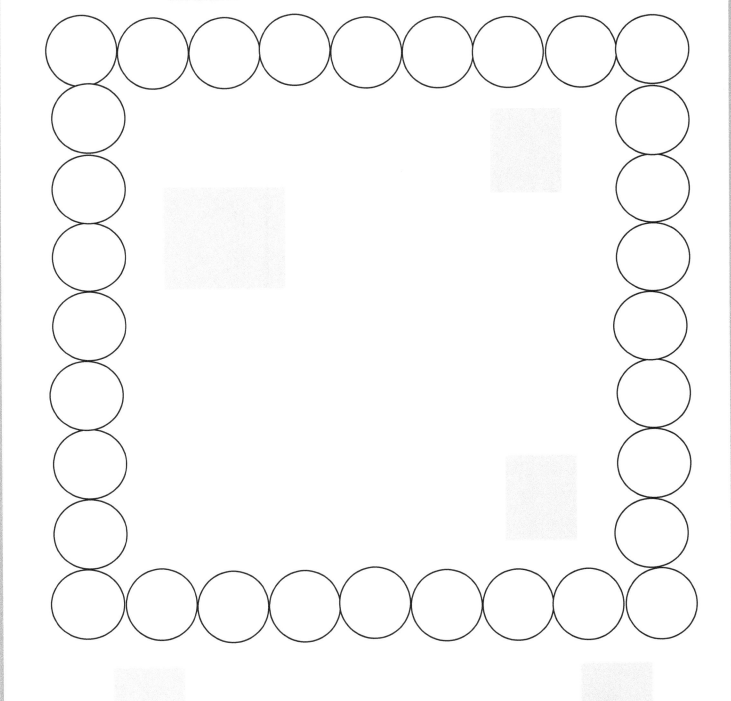

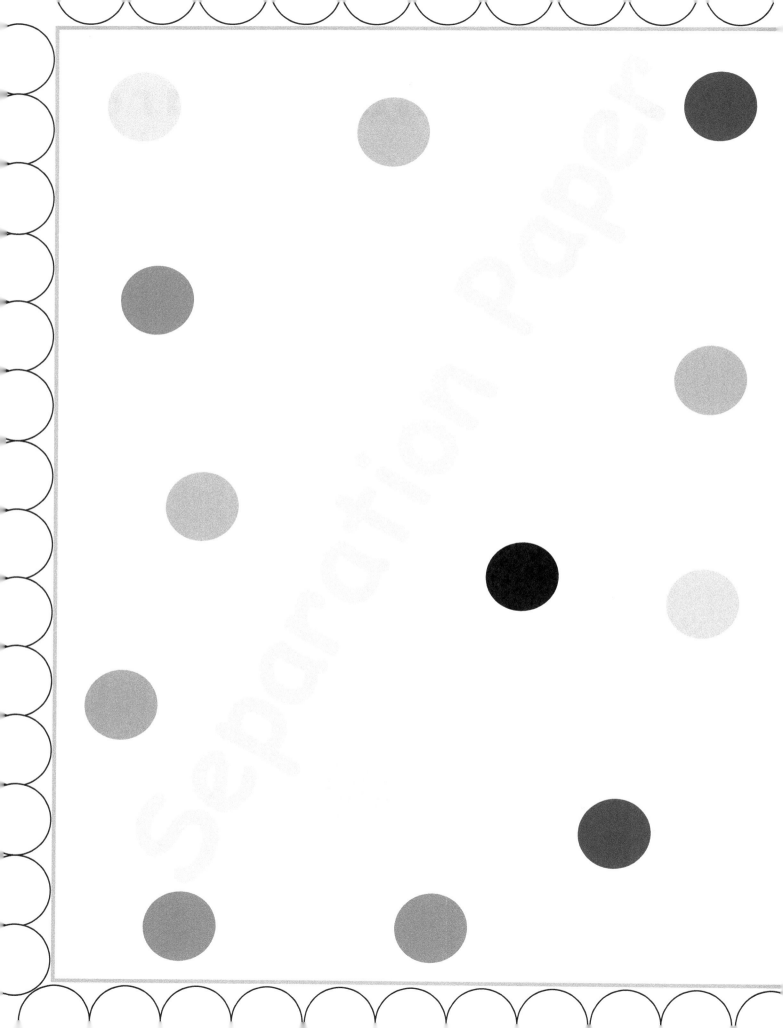

Color the dots inside the shape

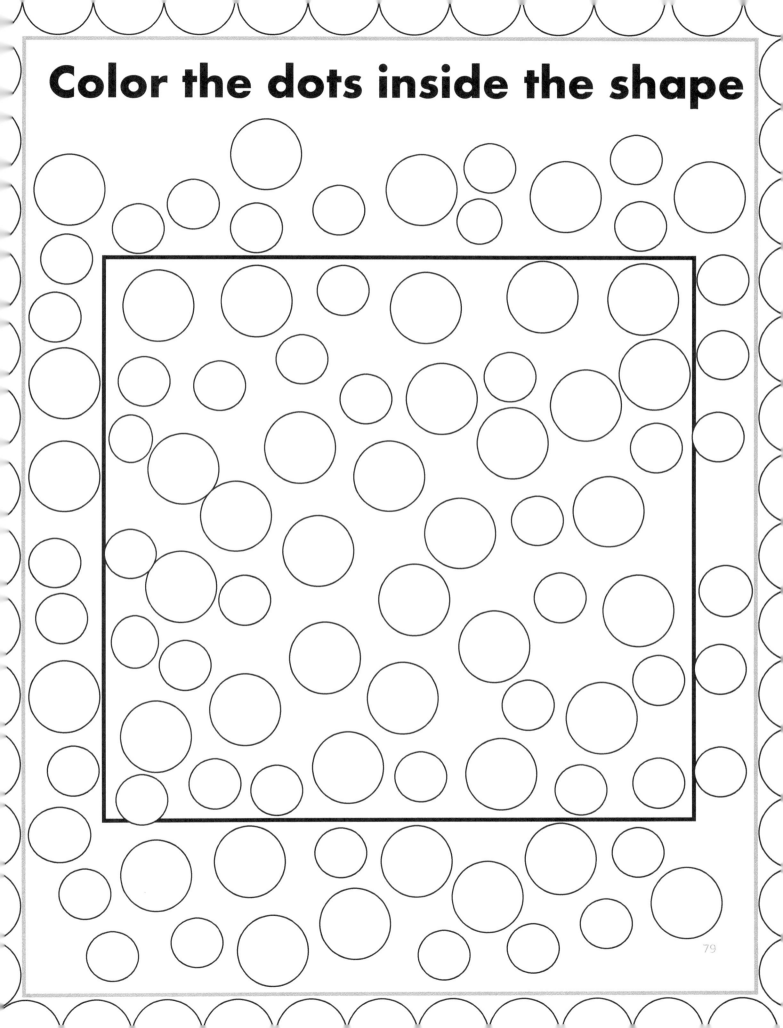

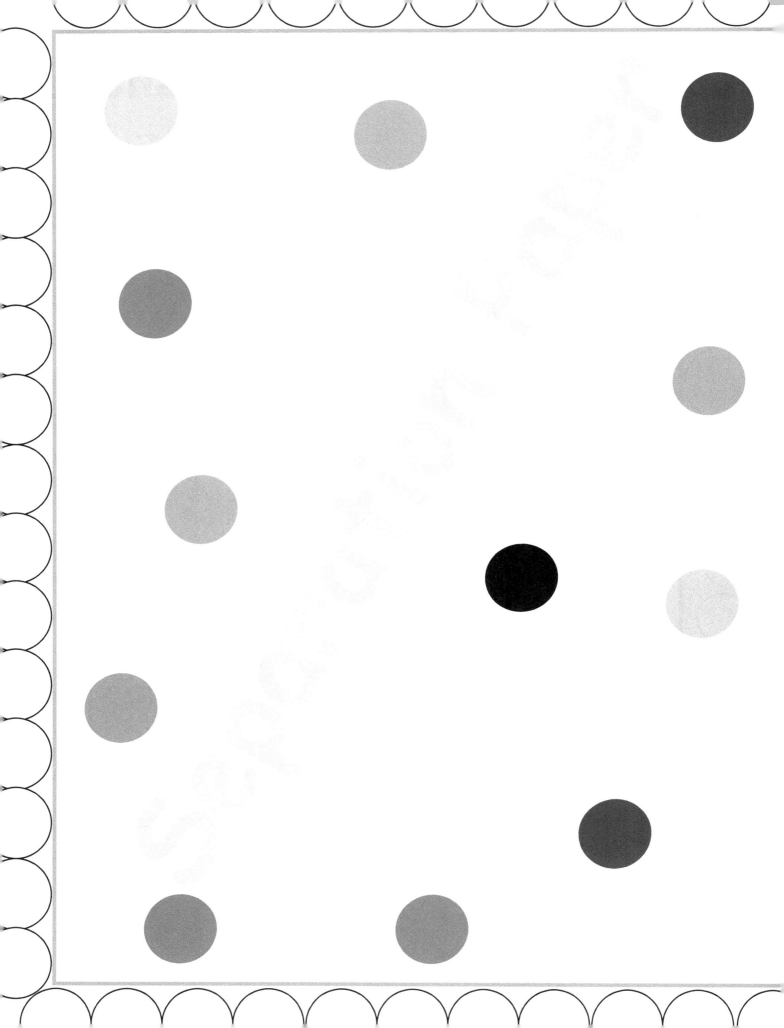

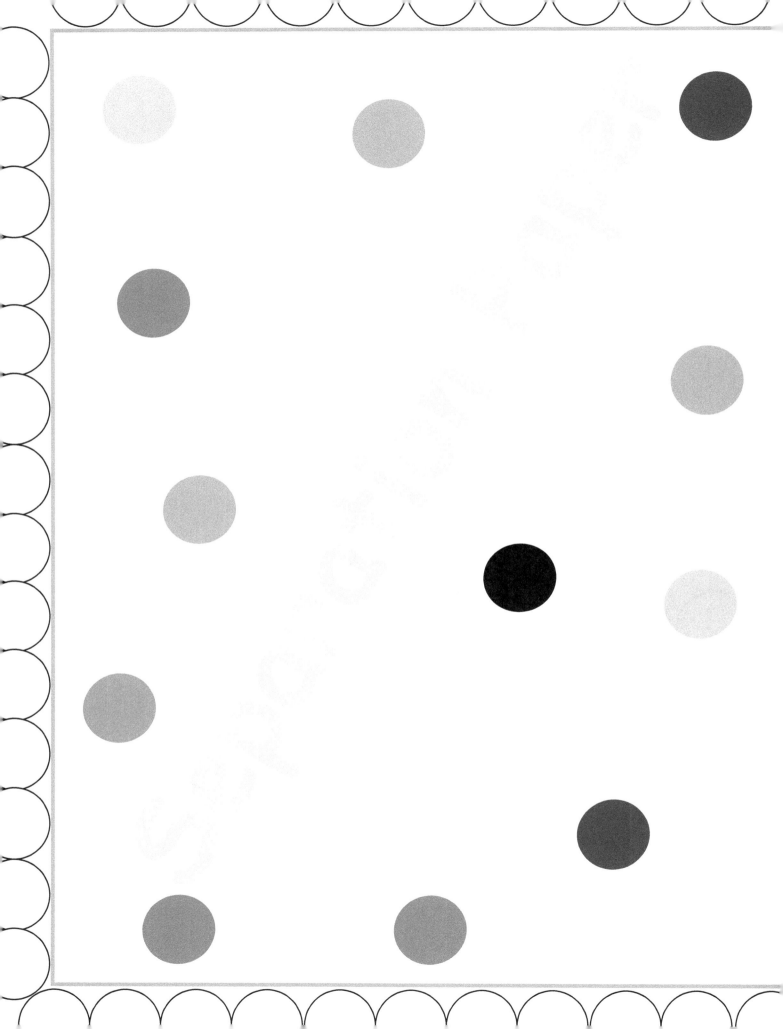

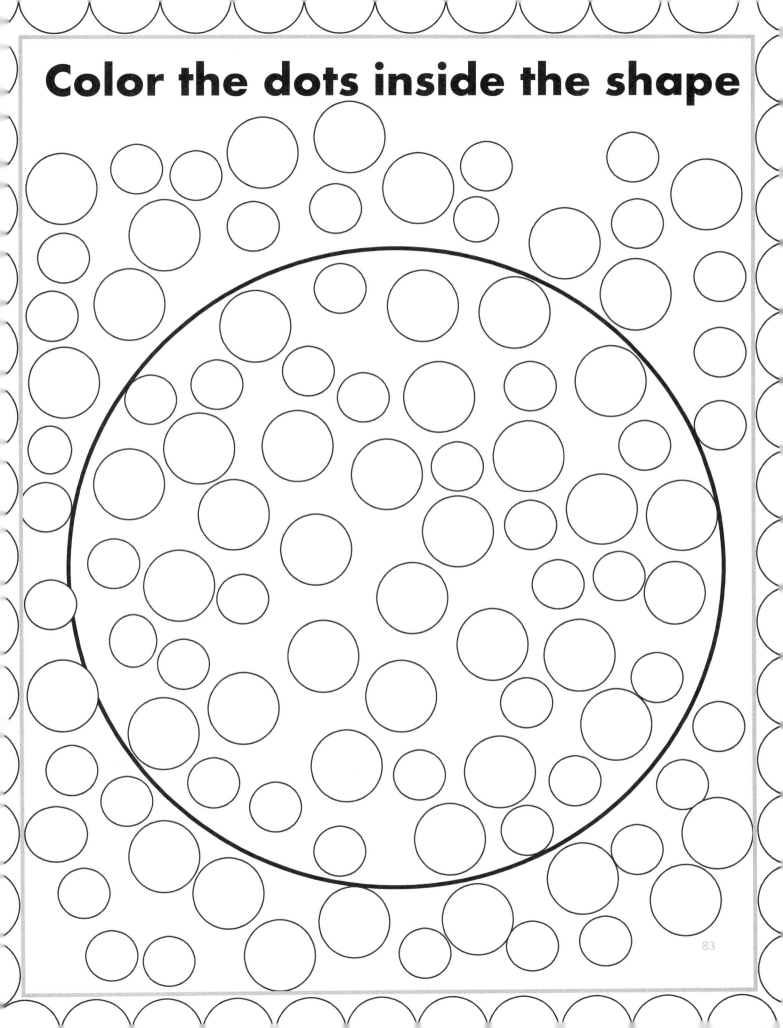

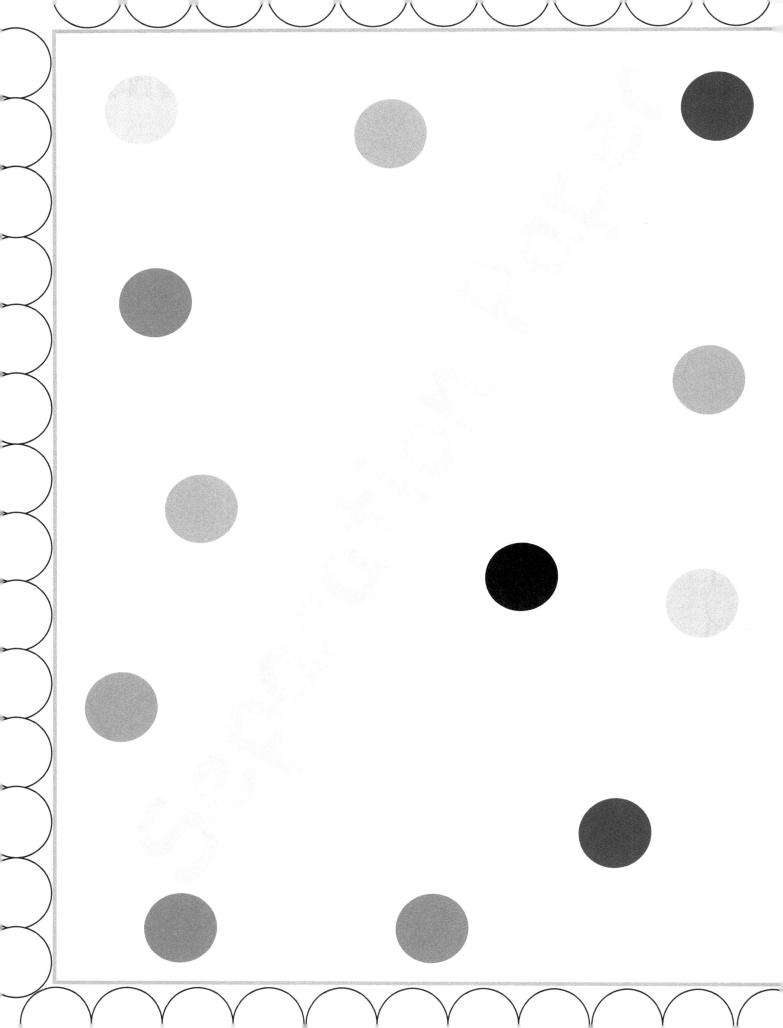

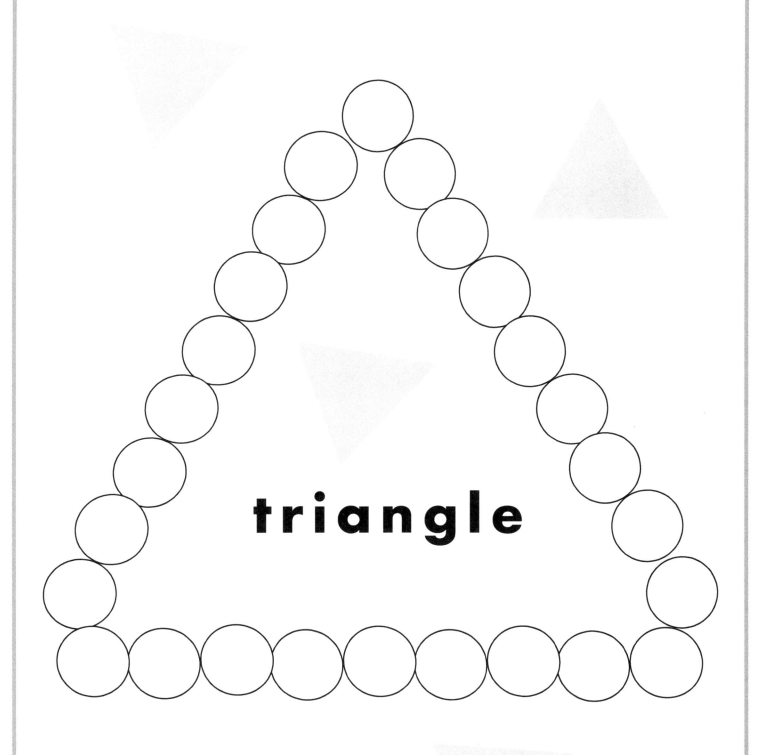

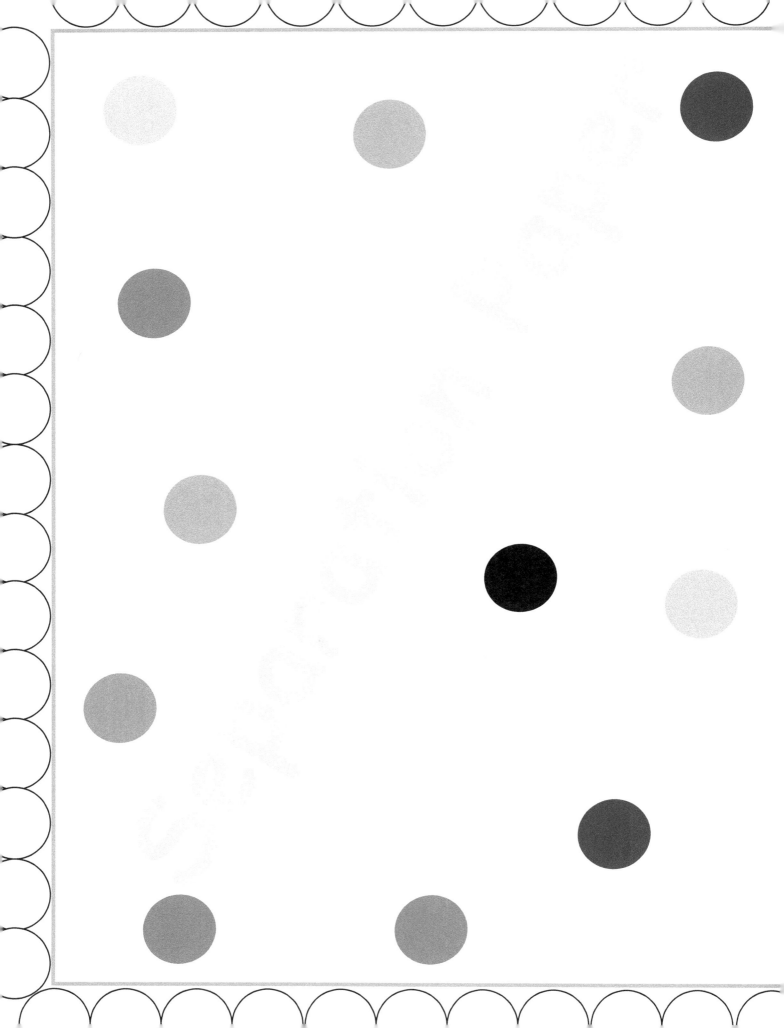

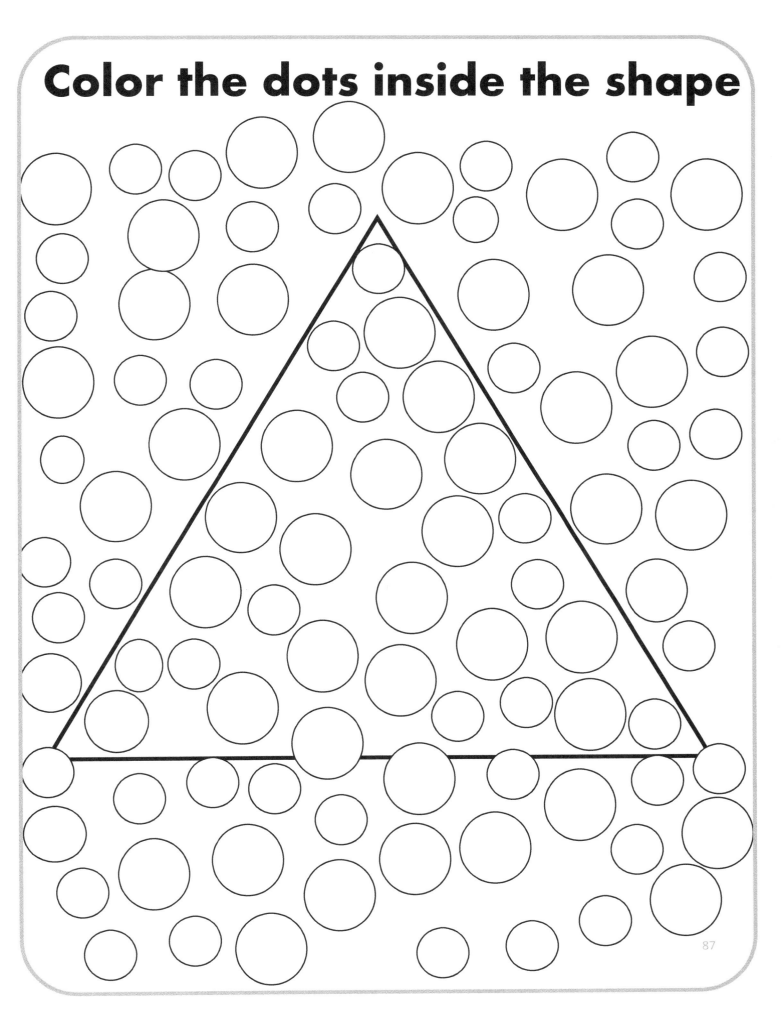

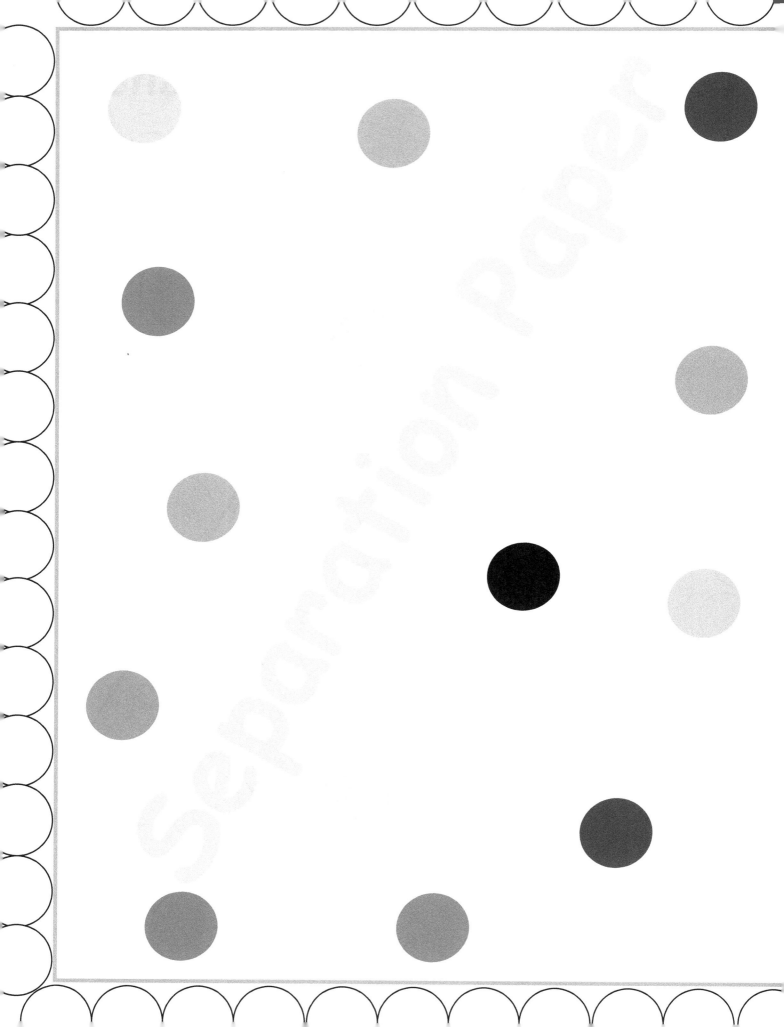

Parallelogram

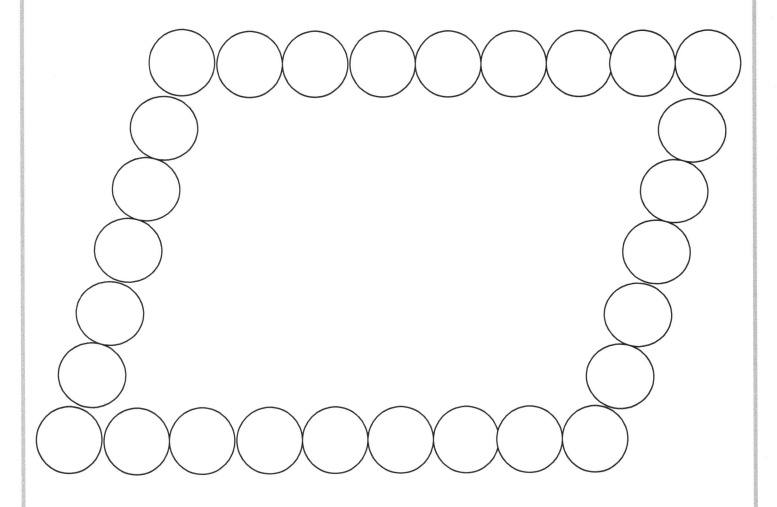

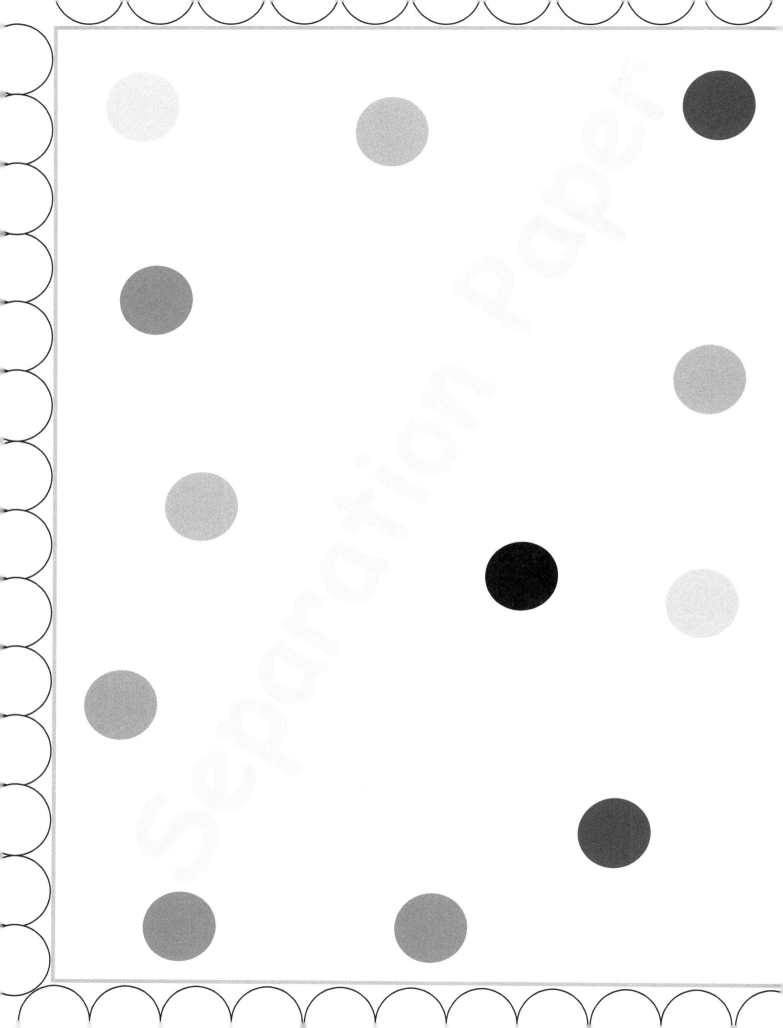

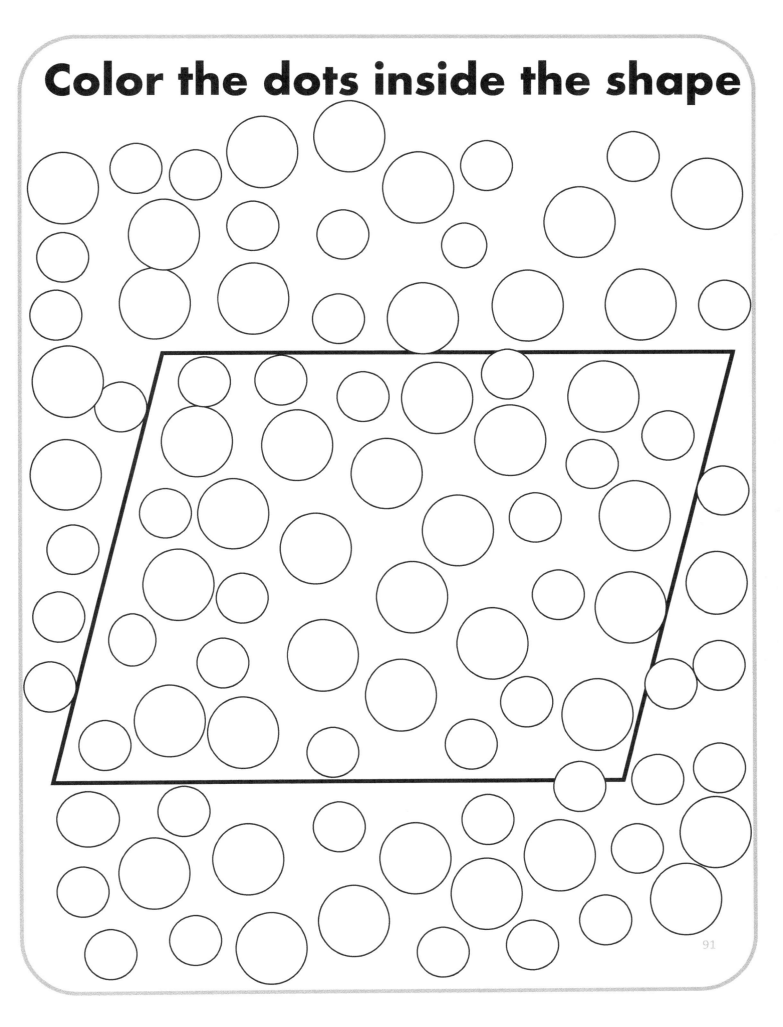

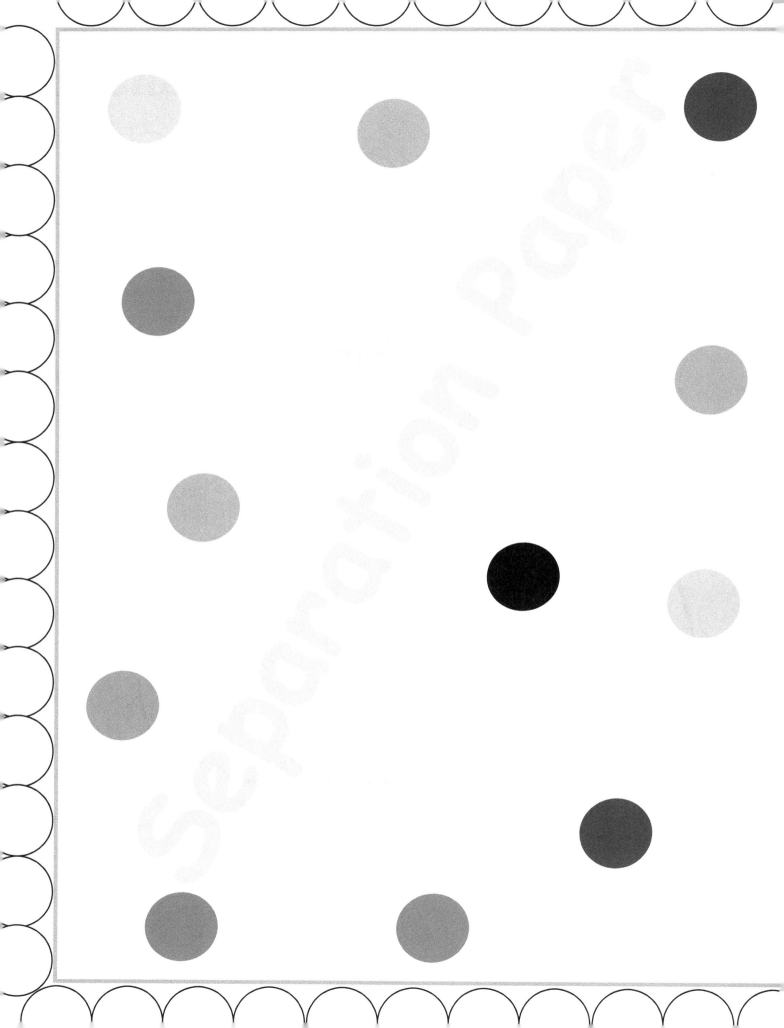

Rhombus

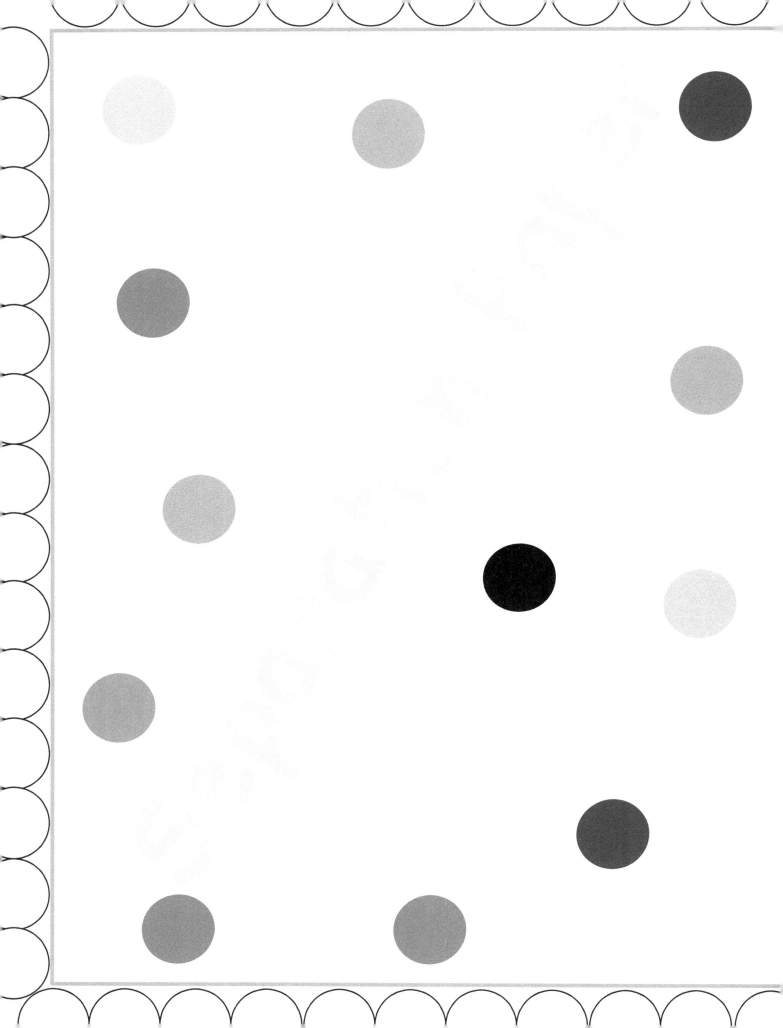

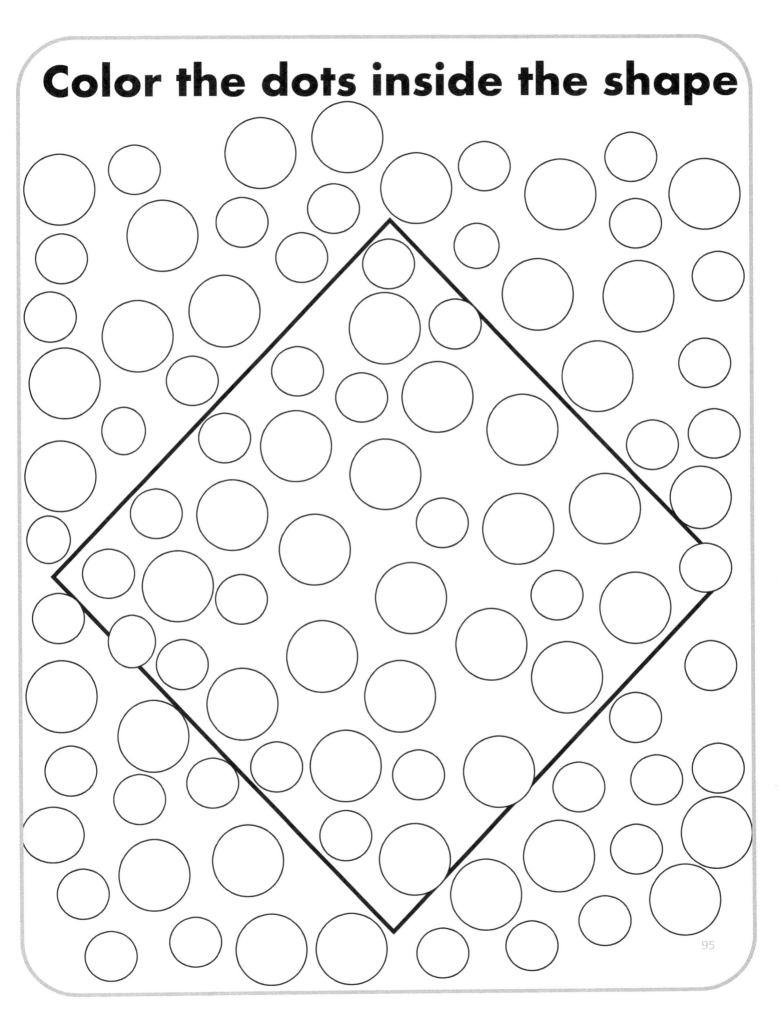

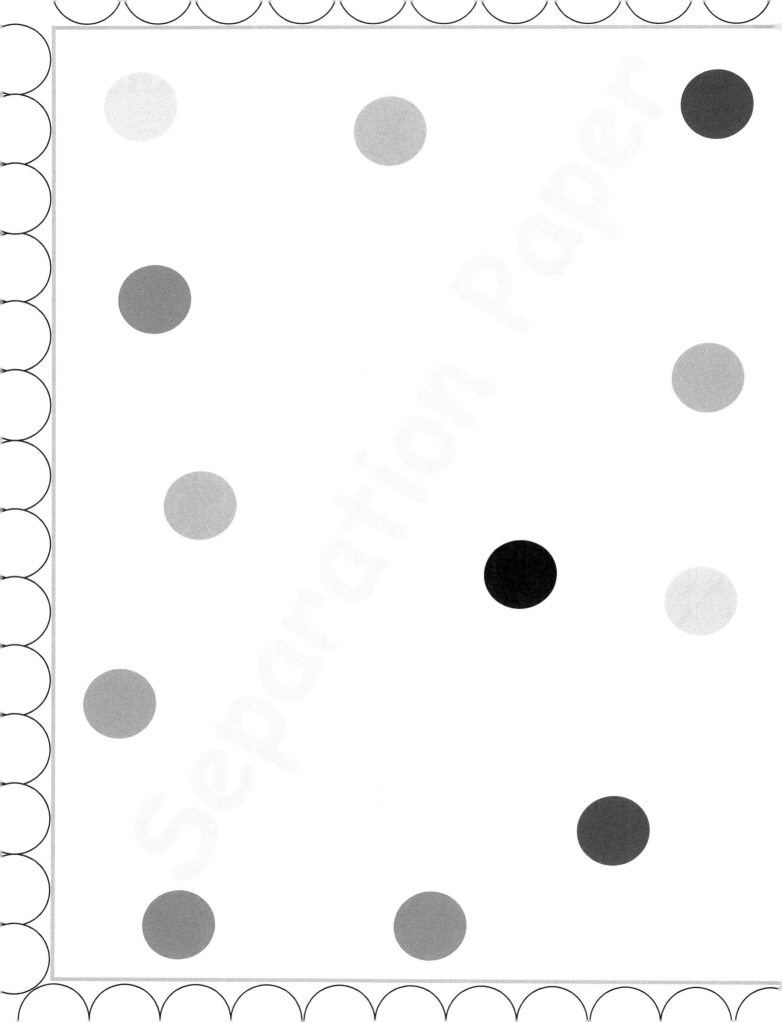

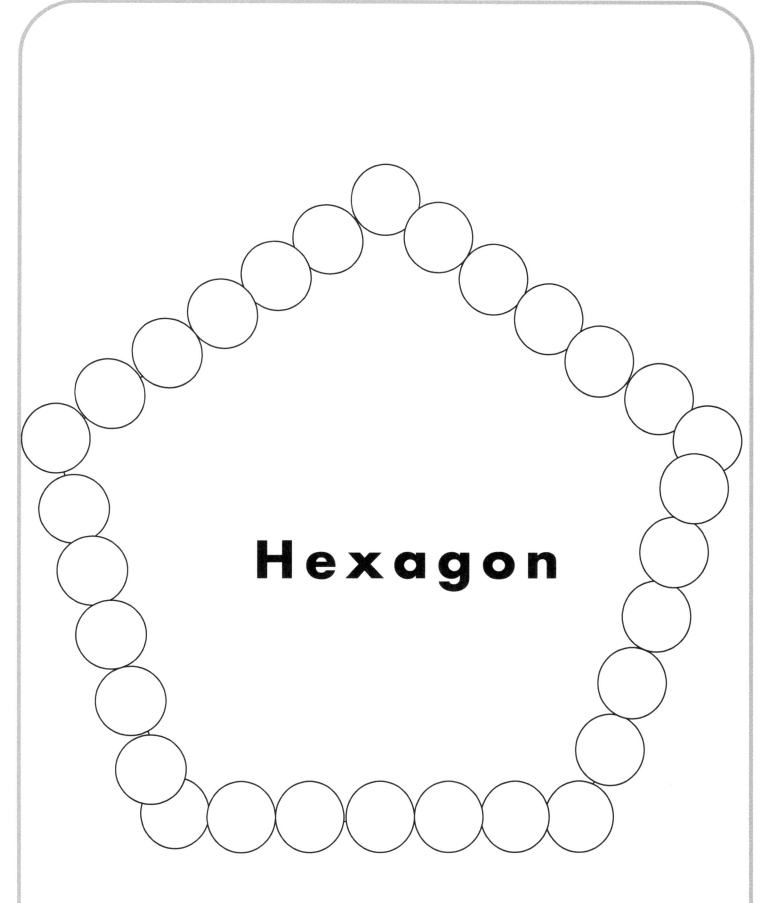

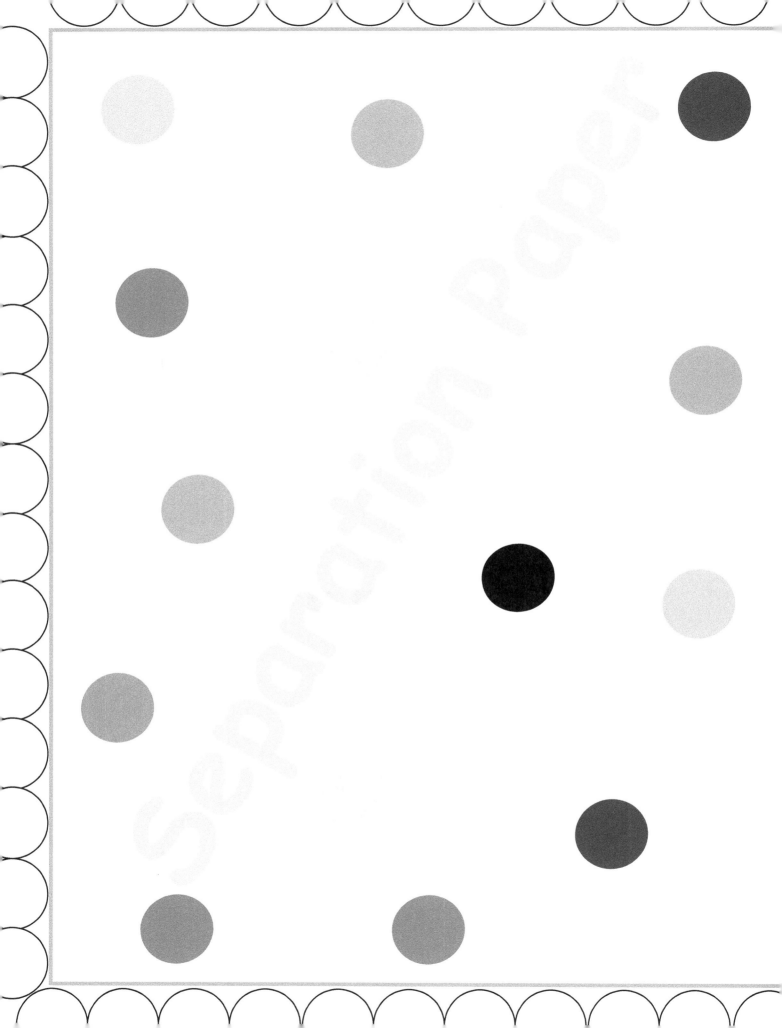

Color the dots inside the shape

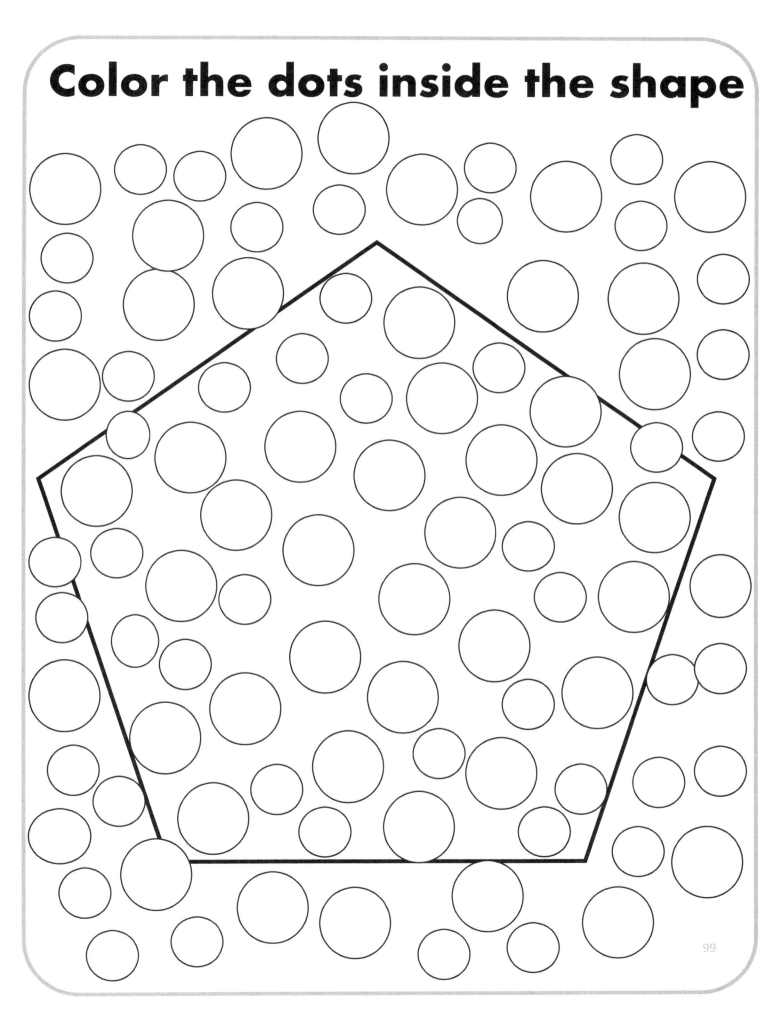

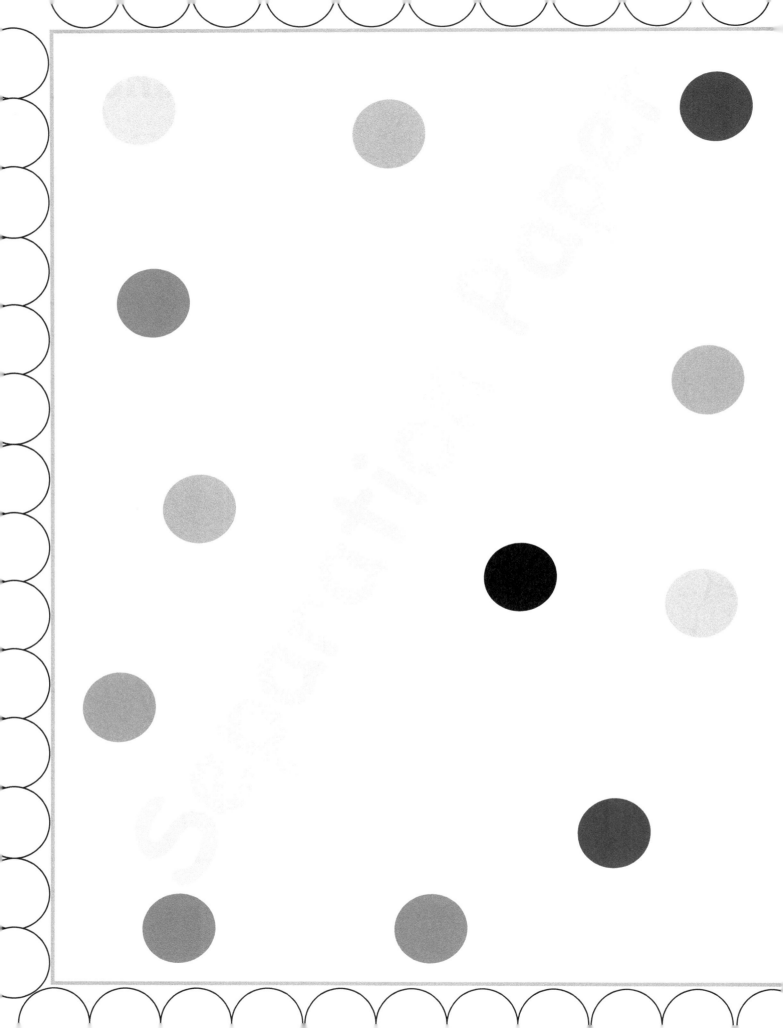

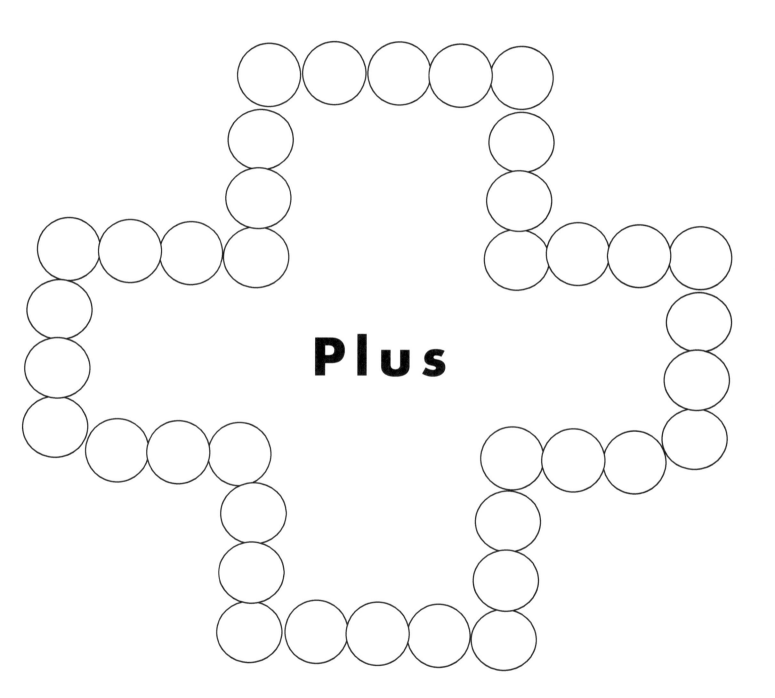

Plus

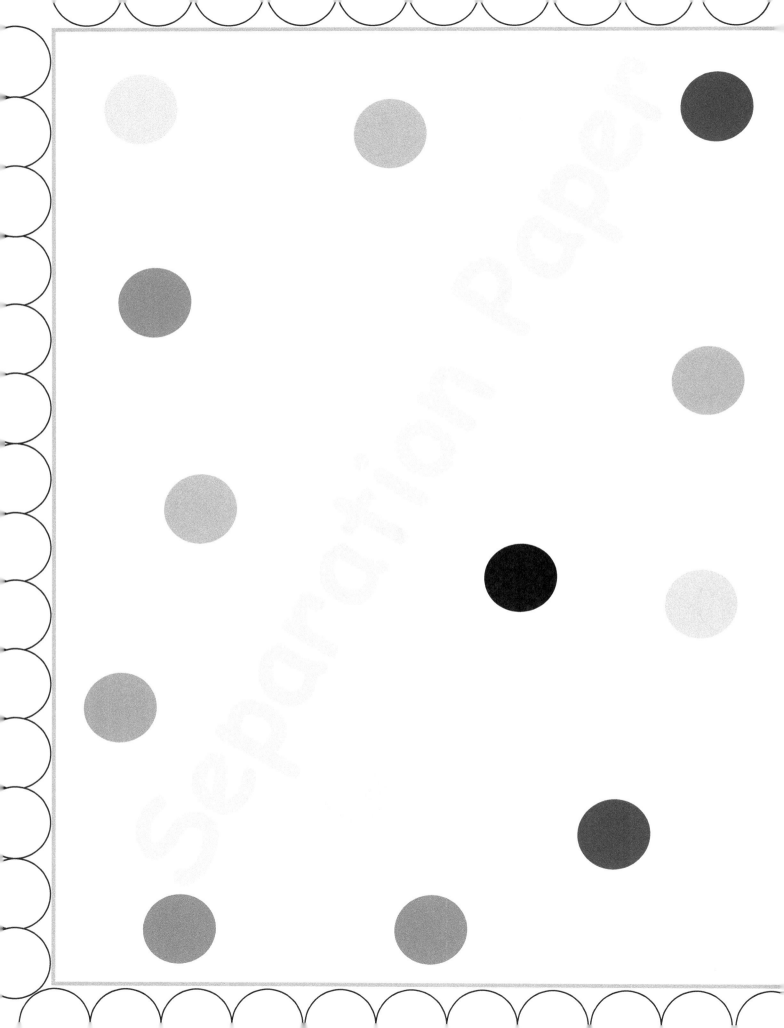

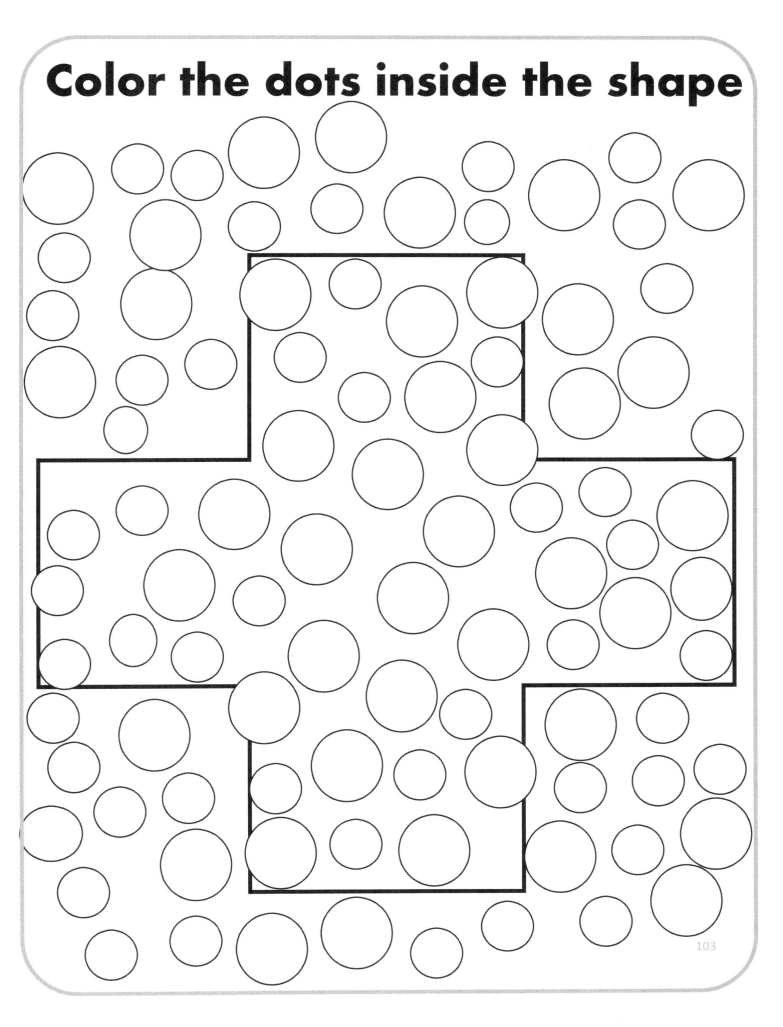

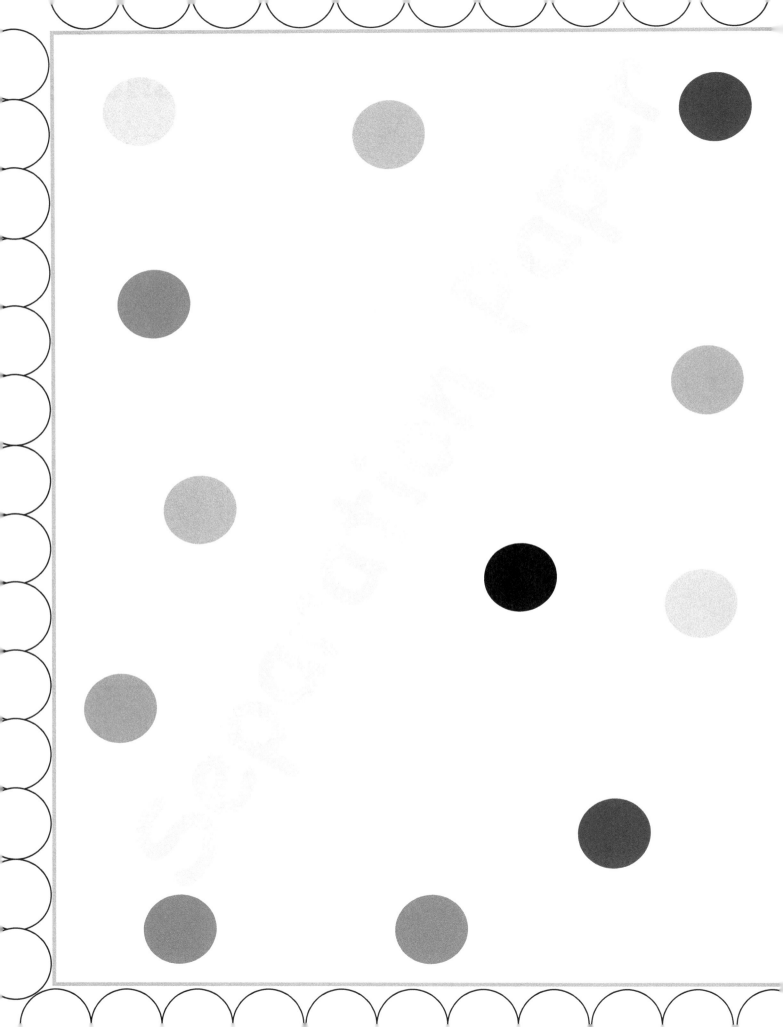

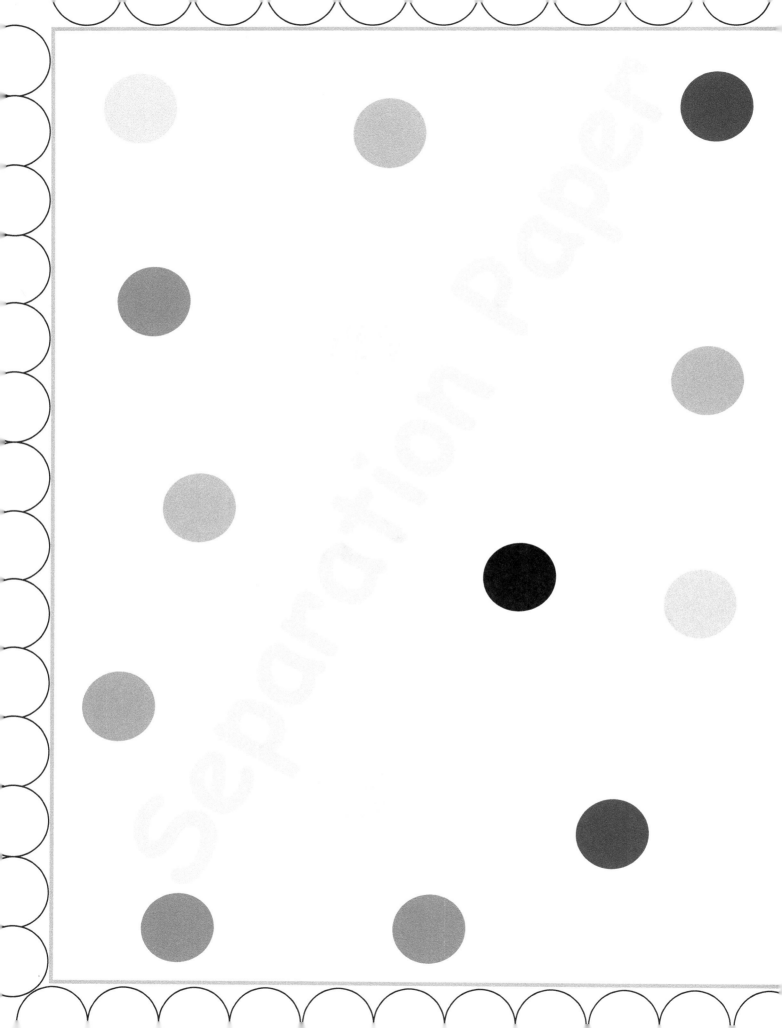

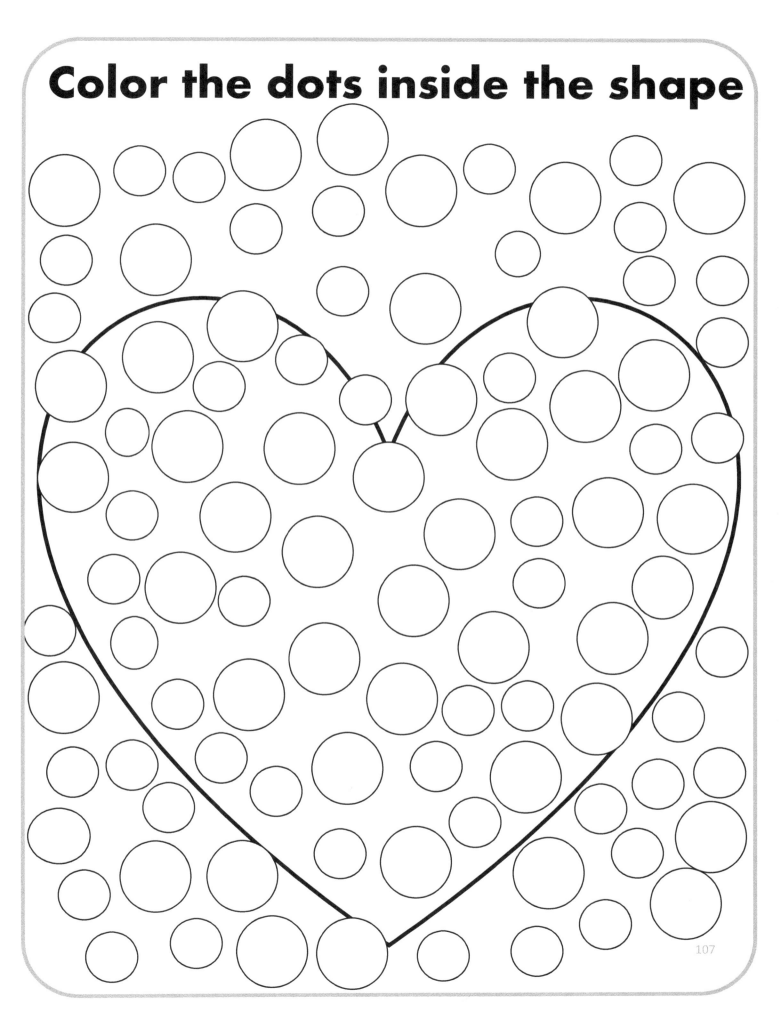

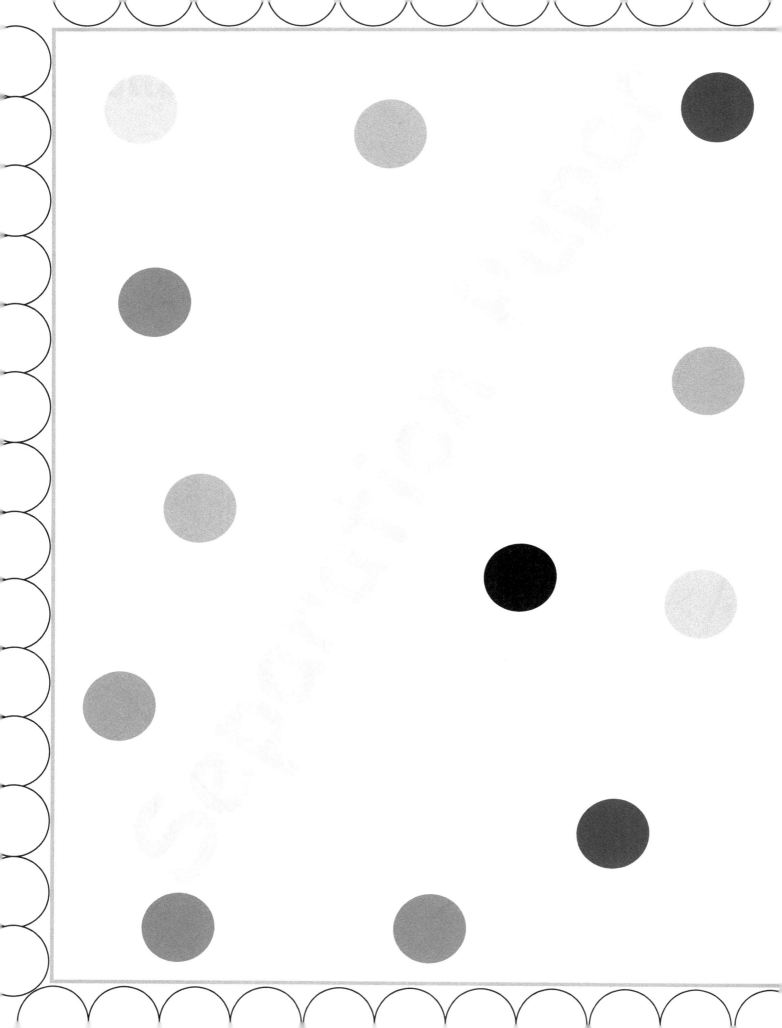

It's the end...!!!!!!!!!!

... GOOD JOB...!!!!!!!!!!

Printed in the USA
CPSIA information can be obtained
at www.ICGtesting.com
LVHW080000141124
796580LV00043B/1746